Ruth Teakle is a wonderful si
a way that inspires new persp
into the Word. The testimoni
always a joy to unpack in my small group! I'm so thankful for these
devotionals.

—*Amie Vandevrie, Vice President ADS MEDIA,*
Hamilton, Ontario, https://adsmedia.ca

I am awestruck reading this well-thought-out devotional on the fruit
of the Spirit. Each section is well-written, with authentic personal stories woven into applicable biblical illustrations, concluding with char-
acter-building truth from the scriptures. I found this devotional to be
incredibly encouraging.

—*Rev. Noral Woodburn, Associate Pastor, BP Church,*
Calgary, Alberta

Embracing Goodness is a heartfelt and inspiring devotional. Oh, how we
need to be reminded daily of the transformative power of God's goodness in the midst of life's questions and challenges! Each daily devotion
resonates with how God leads us through every peak and valley of our
lives, turning our waiting and even our struggles into purpose and fulfillment. You'll be strengthened and encouraged as you read this book!

—*Alvin and Joy Slaughter, Alvin and Joy Slaughter International,*
New York, USA

Uplifting, compact, and heartfelt. Well-written, relatable stories that
helped me clearly see God's goodness in my own life and have inspired
me to reflect that to others. A must-read!

—*Ruth Paul, Administrative Assistant, Kids' Ark International,*
Auburndale, Florida

Embracing Goodness will reveal another wonderful aspect of God's nature
that He wants to share with His children. These daily reminders of God's
goodness shining through ordinary people will warm your heart.

—*Grant Mullen M.D., Author of* Emotionally Free,
drgrantmullen.com

Embracing Goodness is inspirational and encouraging. The testimonies are clearly written and biblically sound. You can expect the truths of these daily readings to touch your heart and motivate Holy Spirit change.

—*Joanne Radke, Manager of Chaplaincy & Prayer Centre Ministries*
CBA/700Club Canada, Author of Why Is My House Always a Mess?: How
to DeClutter & Organize Your Home in Just 30 Days,
Toronto, Ontario

A very worthwhile read. Full of life-changing testimonies. They brought back for me forgotten truths learned as a child, truths that undergirded me in times of great need throughout the years.

—*Cheryl-ann Philip, Managing Director for Truth Nation (Retired),*
Mississauga, Ontario

Embracing
Goodness

Embracing
Goodness

A 30 Day Devotional Journey

Ruth Teakle
& a Company of Friends

EMBRACING GOODNESS
Copyright © 2024 by Ruth Teakle

All rights reserved. Neither this publication nor any part of this publication may be reproduced or transmitted in any form or by any means, electronic or mechanical, including photocopying, recording or any information storage and retrieval system, without permission in writing from the author.

Unless otherwise indicated, scripture quotations are taken from the Holy Bible, NEW INTERNATIONAL VERSION®, NIV® Copyright © 1973, 1978, 1984, 2011 by Biblica, Inc.® Used by permission. All rights reserved worldwide. • Scripture quotations marked (AMP) are taken from the Amplified® Bible, Copyright © 1954, 1958, 1962, 1964, 1965, 1987 by The Lockman Foundation. Used by permission. • Scripture quotations marked (ESV) are taken from The ESV® Bible (The Holy Bible, English Standard Version®). ESV® Text Edition: 2016. Copyright © 2001 by Crossway, a publishing ministry of Good News Publishers. The ESV® text has been reproduced in cooperation with and by permission of Good News Publishers. Unauthorized reproduction of this publication is prohibited. All rights reserved. • Scripture quotations marked (NKJV) are taken from the New King James Version®. Copyright © 1982 by Thomas Nelson, Inc. Used by permission. All rights reserved. • Scripture quotations marked (NLT) are taken from the *Holy Bible*, New Living Translation, copyright © 1996, 2004, 2015 by Tyndale House Foundation. Used by permission of Tyndale House Publishers, Inc., Carol Stream, Illinois 60188. All rights reserved. • Scripture quotations marked (TPT) are taken from The Passion Translation®. Copyright © 2017, 2018, 2020 by Passion & Fire Ministries, Inc. Used by permission. All rights reserved. ThePassionTranslation. com. • Scripture quotations marked (NASB) are taken from the New American Standard Bible®, Copyright © 1960, 1971, 1977, 1995, 2020 by The Lockman Foundation. All rights reserved. • Scripture quotations marked (TLB) are taken from The Living Bible copyright © 1971 by Tyndale House Foundation. Used by permission of Tyndale House Publishers Inc., Carol Stream, Illinois 60188. All rights reserved. The Living Bible, TLB, and the The Living Bible logo are registered trademarks of Tyndale House Publishers. • Scripture quotations marked (VOICE) are taken from The Voice™. Copyright © 2008 by Ecclesia Bible Society. Used by permission. All rights reserved. • Scripture quotations marked MSG are taken from *THE MESSAGE*, copyright © 1993, 2002, 2018 by Eugene H. Peterson. Used by permission of NavPress. All rights reserved. Represented by Tyndale House Publishers, Inc. • Scripture quotations marked (WEB) are taken from the World English Bible, which is in the public domain. • Scripture quotations marked (KJV) are taken from the Holy Bible, King James Version, which is in the public domain. • Scripture quotations marked (CEV) are taken from the Contemporary English Version Copyright © 1991, 1992, 1995 by American Bible Society. Used by Permission.

Printed in Canada

ISBN: 978-1-4866-2544-4
eBook ISBN: 978-1-4866-2545-1

Word Alive Press
119 De Baets Street Winnipeg, MB R2J 3R9
www.wordalivepress.ca

Cataloguing in Publication information can be obtained from Library and Archives Canada.

This devotional is an expression of many shared experiences with the love of my life, my wonderful husband of fifty-six years.

Dedicated to Carl Lavern Teakle, who has taught me what consistent biblical goodness looks like by his integrity, kindness, encouragement, and practical support that remains constant in public and in private. He is a good man who chooses "right," even when it hurts.

I have included some of his stories in this volume.

... Out of the virtue stored in their hearts, good and upright people will produce good fruit ... For the overflow of what has been stored in your heart will be seen by your fruit and will be heard in your words. (Luke 6:45, TPT)

Contents

Getting Started

*But the fruit of the Spirit is love, joy, peace, longsuffering, kindness, **goodness**, faithfulness, gentleness, self-control. Against such there is no law.* (Galatians 5:22–23, NKJV, emphasis added)

*But the fruit produced by the Holy Spirit within you is divine love in all its varied expressions: joy that overflows, peace that subdues, patience that endures, **kindness in action**, a life full of virtue, faith that prevails, gentleness of heart, and strength of spirit* ...(Galatians 5:22–23, TPT, emphasis added)

Goodness originates in God in the same way as love, peace, and every other fruit of the Spirit. He is the source: *"O give thanks to the Lord, for He is good; For His compassion and lovingkindness endure forever!"* (Psalm 107:1, AMP).

Embracing the goodness of God requires a heart that is open and receptive to recognizing His goodness in our lives, and a life that is cultivating a deep and abiding relationship with Him. It also involves a commitment to the life of integrity and honesty, a life that is surrendered and being transformed daily from the inside out. It involves trust and obedience. As we look to who God is and get His perspective on situations, we understand what goodness should look like in our lives. We also gain a restored hope in the continuing power of God's goodness in a fractured world.

Our goodness should be something other human beings can be thankful for, just as we're thankful for the amazing goodness God has shown to us. Goodness is about character—integrity, kindness, generosity, moral courage—and how we treat other people. Goodness prioritizes what God desires.

Our greatest example of the goodness of God is the person and life of Jesus. He revealed the love, priorities, and goodness of the Father in every part of His ministry and ultimately on the cross. His character never changed, even in the face of rejection and brutality. He remained true to who He is.

Biblical goodness lived out often means we too will face resistance or even persecution, but it does what is right regardless of the consequences. It's a work of the Spirit in our lives that strengthens us to live out this kind of goodness, often through benevolent and kind actions.

Based on the psalmist's invitation to *"taste and see"* that the Lord is good (Psalm 34:8), I am inviting you in these daily devotionals to savour some sweet, bite-sized portions of biblical goodness. Each testimony or Bible passage will demonstrate a truth, an outworking, or a reminder of His goodness. Each is authentic and inspiring.

Although we'll only scratch the surface, I pray that you will become hungry for a deeper walk with the Holy Spirit, and that you'll be challenged to cultivate the fruit of goodness in your own life. As Christians, it becomes both *our invitation* and *our responsibility* to spread that goodness to a world that needs to know Jesus. As we accept the challenge, we will live our lives in a manner that welcomes others into a relationship with God so that they can experience His goodness firsthand.

The Unlikely: Encountered by His Goodness

Day One

Your mission is to live as children flooded with his revelation-light! And ... his light will be seen in you—goodness, righteousness, and truth. (Ephesians 5:8b, 9, TPT)

Throughout scripture and history, we see how God has used unlikely people in unlikely ways for His purposes and His glory—women in scripture like Jael, the heroic woman who cunningly killed Sisera; Jochebed, whose faith saved her son Moses; and the youthful Mary, who was chosen to carry in her womb the Saviour of the world. There were also unlikely men, like the timid, hiding Gideon who was called by God to take on the Midianites; David, the shepherd boy God called to be a king; and Saul, the persecutor of the Christians, who later became Paul, the apostle to the Gentiles. Historically, people like Joan of Arc, Harriet Tubman, Catherine Booth, Martin Luther, William Wilberforce, and Mother Teresa come to mind. Their beliefs and priorities were founded upon an ultimate trust in the goodness and faithfulness of God. Each acted upon that trust to choose "right" and change the course of history.

Catherine Booth, for example, was a co-founder of The Salvation Army, a Christian movement committed to preaching the gospel while serving the poor and marginalized in society. She lived out the goodness of God in her own life by preaching, addressing social issues, and opening shelters, soup kitchens, and orphanages for the poor and homeless. She lived a life of prayer and devotion to God, visiting prisons, slums, factories, and mines to share the gospel and offer practical help. Those who knew her report that she was a "good" woman, one of great integrity, focused on serving others.

One of my favourites, however, is the nameless, nondescript woman at the well in Sychar who encountered the goodness and kindness of

God on one of her trips to get water. Her choices in life had brought anguish and disregard. Though blemished with this problematic past, her heart was open to a life-changing revelation (John 4:4–42), and that revelation turned her into one of the least-trained but most effective evangelists of her day.

Jesus was travelling through Samaria on the way to Galilee when He encountered this woman of Samaria. Thirsty and tired, He sat down by the well—Jesus, the breaker of barriers, the carrier of hope, the goodness of God on earth—and asked for a drink. Knowing He was a Jew who was ignoring the religious and social divides, she asked how He could do this. His response was mystifying (v. 10). He offered "*living water*" that would never run dry—and she paid attention. The woman pressed him: "*Sir, give me this water so that I won't get thirsty and have to keep coming here to draw water*" (v. 15).

He then engaged her in a deep and caring conversation, exposing her story—not to shame her but to free her (vv. 17–18). Her eyes were opening to the truth of who He was—Jesus, the Messiah. Spiritual refreshment flooded her soul. He was offering her forgiveness and access to "living water"—eternal life. She left her jug and hurried to tell the townspeople what had happened. Her testimony of His goodness bore witness to the power of His supernatural love and redemption. That testimony stirred many to follow Him and proclaim Him as Saviour.

As you read this, you might realize that you may be one of those unlikely people God wants to use in unlikely ways. The Lord sees your weaknesses and secrets, yet He pursues and loves you. As you encounter His acceptance, and trust His unfailing love, you will be compelled to respond with full surrender to His call to make a difference for His glory.

Heavenly Father, while I see myself in some moments as an unlikely choice to carry your goodness, I choose today to trust you. You have a good plan for me, and I want to grow in your goodness, learning each day to submit to your plan with gratitude and joy. Amen.

Stepping into His Goodness

Day Two

God can bless you with everything you need, and you will always have more than enough to do all kinds of good things for others. (2 Corinthians 9:8, CEV)

Growing up in a family with four children, our parents were challenged monthly to meet expenses. This meant that each of us had to wait our turn for certain things. Mom and Dad worked hard, but there were hungry mouths to feed and bills to pay. Haircuts and dental appointments had long gaps in between. Shoes were in that same category. They were on a "turn-taking" budget. Savings for shoes took time to accumulate, so new shoes, whether needed or not, meant waiting your turn. On a trip to the shoe store, we'd try on whatever was on sale, fit them just right, and then Mom would purchase a pair in the next size up. This was a pre-emptive strike in case your feet grew faster than expected and your shoes began to cause blisters. Turn-taking in shoe purchases assumes, of course, that all of us grew at the same rate! We could dream of having new shoes—the latest style and perfect fit, ones that made us feel comfortable and confident—but that wasn't a luxury we could afford. So whether they were too big or too tight, they had to last until it was our turn.

It took me a while to figure out why, but one of my favourite things to do on our annual mission trips to the Caribbean schools was to bring suitcases full of new running shoes and soccer shoes. While training teachers in a new curriculum and leading drama teams in the schools was exciting, I loved gathering students in the teachers' room to try on the donated shoes and select the ones they liked best. We had every name brand imaginable! I'd smile inwardly as I heard various teachers encouraging their students to choose a size bigger than they needed—advice that sounded vaguely familiar. The soccer shoes, on the other hand, must fit perfectly, because bringing home a trophy from the county soccer matches was a coveted honour.

There's a beautiful justice in heaven's goodness. God will often make good of those places in our history where there was a sense of discomfort or unfairness. The joy of these children choosing new shoes was a picture of His goodness multiplied. While my shoes as a young girl may not have been fancy, or might have pinched or been sloppy, I always had shoes. A number of the schools we visited had hot, black-surfaced play areas, and frequently students with bare feet.

If your past has included a time of waiting your turn, things that didn't fit right, or dreams of something better, you can be sure that God can take that very thing and turn it around for His good. Did you grow up with an absentee father? Allow Him to use you as a father to the fatherless. Did you grow up with sadness and loss? Allow Him to use you to deliver compassion and strength.

He is a God who cares about the details of our lives. In every aspect of His character, He is good. I can remind myself not to be chained to the past and what might have been or might have seemed unfair—God has used it for my good and the good of many others. Any pain or impatience in my waiting has since been far surpassed by the joy of sharing His goodness with others in this practical way, blessing His kids one pair of shoes at a time.

Thank you, Jesus, for your redemptive goodness. I give you my past disappointments and my dreams for the future. I can safely entrust you to work good into every part of my life. Amen.

Watch for My Goodness

Day Three

Contributed by Kerrin Norman

Then Moses asked to see God's glory. The Lord replied, "I will make my goodness pass before you, and I will announce to you the meaning of my name Jehovah, the Lord. I show kindness and mercy ..." (Exodus 33:18–19a, TLB)

I had always been busy. I served the Lord in many ways through our church and was blessed to see the work of His hands in the lives of those I interacted with daily. I loved what I did, but it wasn't uncommon for me to come home exhausted and empty. Friends would readily identify me as vivacious, energized, multitalented, and compassionate. Since I was seeing the fruit of my labours, I never thought to ask questions about whether what I was feeling in my mind and body was normal: numbness, exhaustion, confusion. This was a new spiritual walk for me, and I didn't recognize my need for help. I just kept digging deeper, pushing through, putting a smile on my face, and asking the Lord for strength. This worked ... until it didn't.

I felt blindsided and shaken when I suddenly found myself unable to function. While I hoped it was temporary, the numerous doctors' appointments, tests, and downward spiral didn't confirm either a clear or a speedy solution. Each day was a struggle just to exist, with scary and debilitating symptoms. I made the heartbreaking decision to step back from ministry and focus on my health. I was devastated and wondered what God was up to. On many mornings, His goodness seemed like a distant memory. I knew He hadn't caused this illness, and His Word promised that He wouldn't waste it.

I ran to Him for answers and healing. I didn't get either. When a small ray of light began to break through the fog, what I got was so much better. In the quiet of my forced solitude, His love and goodness offered two invitations. Both were simple and uncomplicated—just what I was able to handle at the time. The first was to look and listen for Him in everything. Though initially doubtful, I chose to take God at His word that every good and perfect gift would come from above (James 1:17). From my bed, I could see how God was loving me. Calls from friends came just when I needed encouragement the most. God was right by my side, showing me how close and involved He was.

The second invitation was to *"look at the birds"* (Matthew 6:25–33). I began to see beautiful birds in our yard. Sometimes it was one I'd never seen before; at other times, it was a whole chorus of the more common ones, sometimes in staggering numbers. Some would come right up to the ledge of the window and stay for longer than normal. Each time I was visited by the birds, I basked in His hope and thanked God for His love.

As He revealed my pattern of striving and its resulting damage, He showed me that I didn't have to keep "doing" to earn the love and acceptance I already had from Him. In the middle of my deepest pain, God's goodness was all around me, without me doing a thing to earn it. And with this revelation, I was undone! It felt like He had lifted a huge weight! I felt free. Seeing His goodness repeatedly pass before me set me free. What an amazing new peace I found in loving Him and being restored to serve from a new place of His love and freedom.

Father, thank you for loving us as we are. The evidence of your goodness is all around us. Open our hearts to see that love—not just for ourselves, but so that we can share your love and goodness with others who may be struggling or feeling overwhelmed in their journey. Amen.

Every Good Thing

Day Four

Every good thing given and every perfect gift is from above, coming down from the Father of lights, with whom there is no variation or shifting shadow. (James 1:17, NASB)

Biblical goodness speaks to both the character of integrity of the one expressing goodness and to the actions carried out. Sometimes we categorize goodness as something weak, a virtue that won't get anyone to the top of the corporate ladder and won't help build the college fund for our kids. In a world that's becoming increasingly harsh, self-interested, and crisis-ridden, can goodness flourish or even survive? Do we have what it takes to do right when the world demands that everyone make his own interests a priority? Throughout scripture, we see that goodness comes to invade the tyranny and re-set the default thinking in unexpected ways. Goodness holds an enormous strength to change hearts, consequences, and even atmospheres. In Mark's Gospel, we read of an encounter between Jesus and a crowd of people within the region of Decapolis:

> *And they brought to Him one who was deaf and had dif-
> ficulty speaking, and they begged Him to lay His hand
> on him. And Jesus took him aside from the crowd, by
> himself, and put His fingers in his ears, and after spit-
> ting, He touched his tongue with the saliva; and looking
> up to heaven ... He said to him ... "Be opened!" And
> his ears were opened, and the impediment of his tongue
> was removed, and he began speaking plainly ... And they
> were utterly astonished, saying, "He has done all things
> well ... "* (Mark 7:32–35, 37a NASB)

How beautifully personal and affirming Jesus was to engage this man face to face. Although a crowd of supporters had come, He didn't respond to them; He responded to the man. He knew him as a person with a past, a person with hurts and with hopes. He saw, as well, how the situation was about to change for one who'd lived his life ridiculed, devalued, and isolated. In that private moment, Jesus communicated and acted with intention, and goodness invaded the expectations and curiosity of the crowd.

Jesus tenderly placed His fingers in the man's ears and then touched them to his tongue. Then He looked up. Don't read too quickly over this particular part. Jesus acknowledges that *every good thing comes from above*. In that moment, *the man is touched by the goodness of Heaven*. This passage reminds me that if we have any goodness to offer the world, it won't be something mustered up from within. It will come from a character built on a yielded and obedient relationship with God, and a heart that has been cultivating the fruit of the Spirit.

If you've ever had a rough day with the kids or difficulties with a co-worker or neighbour who repeatedly gets on your nerves, you know what I mean. Simply trying to be nice in a situation drains your energy and breeds a bitter sense of inadequacy. You'll soon run out of kind words and smiles. You need to tap into His goodness and stay connected to the vine to bear fruit.

Jesus' action changed this man's world. It overcame the hopelessness and heartache, the pain and prejudice. He experienced transformation! As we cultivate His goodness in our hearts, we too can look up and touch others in His name.

Today, Lord, I turn my eyes Heavenward. I confess that any goodness I have comes from you. Teach me to release your goodness with love and confidence. Help me to represent you well. I ask this humbly in your name. Amen.

It Was a Good Christmas ...

Day Five

Do not neglect to do good and to share what you have, for such sacrifices are pleasing to God. (Hebrews 13:16, ESV)

I love the celebrations of the Christmas season. It's always a time of joy, family, gatherings, and belting out the Christmas carols until our voices have stretched beyond their limit. Amid all of that is the challenge of Christmas giving. I recall a Christmas when it was already mid-November, and I had zero gift ideas in mind for the grandparents. During a Saturday shopping trip to the local Walmart, we noticed a special on family photos—promised before Christmas. That was it! We made the booking!

Posing for photos has never been one of my favourite events. But this experience was different. The young gentleman serving us took extra time to chat and ask about our family. He was patient, genuine, and gracious, using our names often. It was customer service at its finest! As we were finishing up, he said, "You don't recognize me, do you?" Of course, we didn't.

He gave his first name and began to share. We were speechless! He told us how Carl, my husband, used to pick him up on a bus for Sunday school in Niagara Falls. He described the small, rundown cottage where he lived and gave the address. He went on to share that one Sunday Carl gave him a Bible. "I was so proud of that Bible," he continued. "My parents weren't really into the church thing, but they were always happy to get me out of the house. The Bible was rejected, so I kept it under my pillow. I started reading it, and I read it every night." After a couple of years, the family moved, and Sunday school vanished. "But I didn't stop reading my Bible. When I was a teenager, I found a church, and I still read that same Bible."

By this point, we were so moved it was hard to think about photos. His job in the photo area was simply a holiday gig to earn extra money for his final year at college. I affirmed him and told him that it was certainly exciting to hear this story. "Yes," he responded, "and the college I'm doing is Bible college!" What an amazing celebration we enjoyed together. We held back the tears until we reached the car, but it was a beautiful moment of gratitude and praise. In that moment, we saw the unfolding goodness of God. His goodness allowed our congregation to purchase that bus. His goodness stirred the heart of that young boy to keep reading the Word and then called him and equipped him for ministry. It was the sweet goodness of God that allowed us to hear the story.

I realize as well that it was the Holy Spirit who stirred Carl to get up early every Sunday, brush the snow off that bus, gas it up, and pick up a couple of dozen wild and energetic kids on each Sunday-morning run. He did this with integrity and selflessness. We don't know how many of those lives were changed, but I think on that Saturday in Walmart, God gave us a peek into Heaven's joy. What a blessing there is in submitting in hiddenness with a pure heart to His invitation to serve. God can take what may seem routine or small and use it to bring glory to His name.

Lord Jesus, my heart is stirred as I consider how you use the small sacrifices in our lives to do big things in light of your kingdom. Help me to humbly serve others and allow you to multiply the impact for your glory. Amen.

Balcony People

Day Six

I am fully convinced, my dear brothers and sisters, that you are full of goodness. You know these things so well you can teach each other all about them. (Romans 15:14, NLT)

Although I've downsized my colossal and cherished book collection over recent years, I have retained my small, lacey, flowered copy of a book titled *Balcony People* by Joyce Landorf Heatherley. The theme of the pages is focused on the lethal poison of rejection and the healing antidote of affirmation. Joyce contends that seeing and affirming good in other believers builds a bond in love that can be life-changing. People who choose to see good in others often become their cheerleaders and encouragers. She strategically brands these, "balcony people."

Barnabas—Son of Encouragement—one of the leaders in the early Jerusalem church, is an authentic example of a balcony person. He was *"a good man, full of the Holy Spirit and faith ..."* (Acts 11:24). Barnabas was generous with his possessions (Acts 4:37), showed a kind spirit (Acts 9:27), and was godly in his character (Acts 11:24).

Barnabas lived during the time when Saul was terrorizing the followers of Jesus in Jerusalem, taking many as prisoners. Numerous believers lost their lives, including Stephen, one of the first ordained deacons in the early church. Then came that powerful Damascus Road experience where Saul had an exceptional encounter with Jesus and a conversion. Though Saul began to preach Jesus in the synagogues around Damascus and in Jerusalem, *some* Jews wanted him dead. They were all afraid of him, and with good reason! How could they know he wasn't faking it? He could turn on them next!

"*But Barnabas*"! (Acts 9:27). Barnabas had gained an outstanding reputation in Jerusalem. *His character was above reproach.* He was *a good man.* Barnabas became Saul's friend, and he co-signed for Saul with his own name and reputation as the assurance that Saul could be trusted. So Saul moved about freely in Jerusalem, speaking boldly in the name of the Lord. Since some were still dubious, however, he was sent to Tarsus for his own safety.

During Saul's earlier rampage of persecution, many believers had been scattered as far as Antioch. When the Jerusalem church heard of the revival in Antioch, where even Gentiles were becoming believers, they sent Barnabas there. Then he travelled over two hundred miles to Tarsus to persuade Saul to join him in Antioch. Together for the next year they met with the Antioch church and accomplished a great work.

Balcony people believe change, with God's help, is possible. Soon Saul became Paul, the great missionary to the Gentiles and the rest of the world. Without Barnabas, the story may have been quite different. It all happened because Barnabas kept his heart right before God and stood on the balcony and said: "Keep going; you can do it."

I've had many balcony people in my life. Each of them carried a measure of God's goodness that was poured out to me. None were perfect people, but they knew how to cultivate the fruit of the Spirit in their lives, and they modelled that. Each one has had a part in teaching me to value character over gifts and believe that God in me is bigger than my weaknesses. Balcony people nourish our spirits with their encouragement. They value, invest, and live with integrity, choosing to do the right thing even when it's hard. They show kindness, and they don't judge. It's easy to see a bucket-load of God's goodness in them, and *that* goodness gives us a better perspective and faith to keep going!

Jesus, help me to affirm others with the truth about how the Father sees them, and to model your goodness generously and with great faith so that I too can cheer others on.

There's Goodness in the House

Day Seven
Contributed by Mark and Nicolette Cullen

So then, as we have the opportunity, let us do good to everyone, and especially to those who are of the household of faith. (Galatians 6:10, ESV)

Houses hold a place of purpose in the plan of God. There was the house of Zaccheus, where Jesus showed up to set a sinner free. There was the home of the Shunammite woman, who housed a travelling prophet and enjoyed a miracle. In the home of Judas, Ananias laid hands on Saul and saw the restoration of his sight and the infilling of the Holy Spirit. When we consider the goodness of God in our lives, our home is the place where we can testify to God's goodness expressed. It has been a place of welcome for life groups and family events, a refuge, and a place of restoration. It has served to bring hope and comfort.

For six years, we had the opportunity to bless a child through the Fresh Air Fund organization for two weeks each summer. While living with us, she had the opportunity to experience life beyond the inner city of the Bronx. She became another daughter to us, learned to ride a bicycle, went camping, and, most importantly, learned about the love of Jesus.

For several months, a family member's five children resided with us while the youngest was receiving treatment for leukemia. We enrolled them all in school with our daughters. It was such a special time of bonding as we spent nights camping out on the basement floor, praying together, and contending for healing for their brother.

One cold, wintery night, a very frightened woman showed up at our door, clothed in pyjamas, needing acceptance and a safe place. God used us to bring His love to quiet her heart and find her some help.

Our home was opened when friends, contemplating a move from Japan to Ontario, needed a place to stay. They resided with us for a number of months, and this blessing of reconnection has brought us to a lifelong friendship.

God's use of our home for His purposes became life-altering when a courtroom judge ruled we would have, indefinitely, the kinship of our three young grandchildren, all in diapers at the time. "Lord, how will we manage? How will we afford this? I'll have to give up work. We're at a point of independence, with our children in school. We don't have the energy to keep up with the demands of three little ones and still provide quality time and support to our girls."

But God. His goodness was ever-present as the months passed. Even in the immense strain it put on us and our daughters, we grew in His goodness. Looking back, we're so grateful for the opportunity God gave us to sow into their lives and teach them about the love of Jesus in the brokenness and uncertainty of their lives. The close relationship we share with them today wouldn't be possible without the hardship.

God has expanded the walls of our home and our hearts in order for us to trust and honour Him in all that we do. God has provided this place for blessing others and demonstrating His goodness. He has sustained us through each season. We will continually give praise for the goodness of God.

I ask today, Lord God, that you expand the walls of my heart and home to show the goodness you have showered upon me. You are a faithful, unfailing Father and can be trusted to watch over every detail of my life. I lift my praise to you. In Jesus' name. Amen.

Goodness and Generosity

Day Eight

Command them to do good, to be rich in good deeds, and to be generous and willing to share. (1 Timothy 6:18)

Generous giving is the outflow of all who give themselves first to the Lord. A personal response to God's goodness to us brings with it practical expression.

A number of years ago, a friend of ours introduced us to a Salvation Army centre in Ontario called Hope Acres. The facility is a long-term residential rehab treatment centre for up to thirty-six men with substance dependence and concurrent disorders. While visiting the center, we were introduced to some of the clients, who chatted with us about various practical programs in which they participated as they addressed their personal struggles.

We were quite taken with one of the younger men sitting alone in the lounge on a well-loved sofa with his guitar. His voice was angelic and refined. He was obviously finding rest and peace in the melodies and words. The guitar, on the other hand, had seen better days. One string and some frets were missing, the bridge was glued, the outer frame was dented, scratched, and signed in marker by a few too many people who were likely a distance from sobriety at the time. When he caught a glimpse of us, he stopped and offered a rather shy hello. When we commented on his voice, he said that singing and writing songs was one way that he was getting closer to God.

When we left the facility, we couldn't shake the thought that there was something more we should do. Since both my husband and dad had a guitar, the two of them began a problem-solving, Spirit-led conversation. Both had been blessed with their guitars through the kindness of others. While either of them would have given up their guitars in a heartbeat, they felt the Lord prompting them to pool their money and purchase a new guitar for the young man. That would mean a much greater sacrifice, as neither had more than what would make ends meet at the time. No one would have argued that they'd done a "good" thing if they just offered their own guitar. But the integrity of heart matters. They knew the "right" thing to do.

After a trip to the music store a few days later, where faith, favour, and an unexpected promotional sale afforded them the purchase of a shiny new guitar, they headed back to Hope Acres. The joy on my dad's face when they returned from the trip was worth it all. My husband, Carl, continues to recall it as a true God encounter in so many ways. He reminds me that when the Holy Spirit instructs, we have every reason to believe God's already figured out the details.

In New Testament times, the question of our giving to Him is taught as a privilege and a delight. We're exhorted to give cheerfully and with gratitude (2 Corinthians 9:7). Heaven's mathematical calculations are quite different than ours—God has more than enough, but we get to "share" what He has given us.

The widow's gift (Luke 21:1–4) teaches us that there are no excuses for not giving in the manner that He asks. All that we have is His, and we are His stewards. As we cultivate the fruit of the Spirit in our lives, genuine love for the Lord will move us to actual acts of love toward others. Goodness is that rightly ordered motivation that prioritizes what God desires. The result? We have the joy of knowing that our response has played a small part in helping someone else find freedom and hope.

Dear Lord Jesus, I want to be a good steward of everything you've placed in my life. Fine tune my hearing to Heaven's call for clear direction, and strengthen my heart to obey so that I too may know the joy that comes from giving freely. Amen.

Restored by His Goodness

Day Nine
Contributed by Randy Cockhead

They will utter the memory of your great goodness, and will sing of your righteousness. (Psalm 145:7, WEB)

Dan was our younger son and only six months old when Diane and I were informed of his medical condition. A bone in his skull had fused, and he would need surgery to repair it. This was only the beginning. We had little sense of what lay ahead—the cycle of surgeries and painful hospital visits that would continue for years. As I watched nurses roll the hospital bed into the elevator with my little boy, who was crying and reaching out to my wife, I suddenly realized how ill-equipped I was for fatherhood.

Throughout this ordeal, my mother constantly told me that she and the church were praying for us. In my frustration and bitterness, I dismissed her and let her know that I had things under control. How did my son's pain fit the picture of God's goodness? I wasn't interested in her prayers. My disappointment with God seemed irreparable, and with what seemed to be good reason. His investment in me seemed anything but good. At ten, my father died of a heart attack while cleaning our church. My friends were few. Most significant males in my life were hurtful and uncaring. I was angry with God and the church, and with my father for dying. I wanted nothing to do with it. I was drowning in grief and didn't trust God or people, especially men.

At the age of four, Dan required another surgery, as things hadn't developed as desired. In a risky twelve-hour procedure, a team of surgeons would attempt to remove his forehead and orbital bones and reshape them for permanent growth. I'm not sure we had looked fear in the face to this extent in any part of the journey with Dan.

When surgery day arrived, Diane and I waited in a very crowded waiting room; we couldn't even get seats together. As time passed, I found myself overcome with both fear and hopelessness. I had nothing within to help my son or comfort my wife. My mother's constant reminder that she and the church were praying reverberated in my pounding head. I thought to myself, *Maybe I should try to pray, even though I'm mad at God.* Without really knowing how to proceed, I began to tell God about my fears and desires in this situation. I felt what seemed to be a physical embrace and a voice that said, "He will be all right." It was so tangible that I had to look up to see if it was Diane or a volunteer, but there was no one nearby. I was shaken. Following a successful surgery, Dan was released, incredibly, in less than a week.

Even now, as I reflect on this powerful visitation of the Lord when I had rejected Him and judged His love, I recognize that the promise He spoke wasn't just for my son but also for the broken little boy who had prayed it. It was a new beginning, a restored relationship.

The love of God has brought healing to my heart. He has proven Himself trustworthy and good in my life. He has freed me from my anger against my dad, the church, and most importantly, Him. He has blessed me with many good men—pastors, mentors, and friends to me. They have modelled His goodness for me and encouraged me as I have pursued Christlikeness and integrity in my own life. We have declared His word, "He will be all right," many times over our two now-grown sons, over my health journey, over jobs, losses, and other challenges. He has remained faithful and good.

P.S. Do I need to admit that sometimes mothers really do know best?

Father, your Word is truth. It is peace and comfort to our spirits, and life to our wearied hearts. There is no greater love than yours. You are such a good God! I give you praise. Amen.

The Real Jesus

Day Ten

Contributed by Wade Sanderson

And we know that God causes all things to work together for good to those who love God, to those who are called according to His purpose. (Romans 8:28, NASB)

I am a Treaty Six Indigenous man whose mother was sent to residential school from ages seven to nine years old. While she wasn't one of the many who suffered abuse during her time at the school, the trauma of forced separation, being taken from her family at a young age, was painful. She was unable to see her parents for those years, with no explanation except government orders.

Generations of Indigenous children were abused under the mandate of the government motto: "Kill the Indian, save the man." Thousands didn't make it out alive. My mother, like many others, suffered from generational trauma. She and my father became severe alcoholics. My dad left when I was young, and my mom's addiction continued. I was taken into foster care at age seven, for more than a year, and I remember trying to run away.

I became an alcoholic after high school. A single drink eventually led to a near fatal addiction. While riding home to our community in northern Saskatchewan after a weekend of partying, a voice spoke to me in my Cree language and told me to put my seatbelt on. In my drunken state, I managed to do so before passing out. I realized years later that it was the voice of God that saved my life that day. A few minutes later, the truck flipped. When I came to, my head was bleeding.

But the nightmare outside the truck was unbearable. My best friend was crushed under the vehicle and lost her life. The shock caused me to stop drinking, but only for a few weeks. A subsequent vehicle accident occurred with me driving drunk at the wheel, almost killing an older couple. It's only by the grace of God that no one was hurt. I lost my license and my job, and I was hopeless.

Around that time, revival was breaking out in my community. I was invited to a tent meeting where the gospel was being preached. I decided to give it a try. The presence of God was so strong in that tent that I began to weep. It was like the liquid love of Jesus pouring all over me. I was experiencing true love for the first time in my life. I wanted the relationship with the Jesus that the preacher was talking about. I responded, and my life was forever changed that night. The goodness of God visited me in my pit of hopelessness. I wept in His presence for days. I started sharing the love of Jesus with others right away. He has kept me and helped me to grow strong in my faith. Now I can give the love and power of Jesus away to others trapped in darkness.

We're now walking through a challenging season of truth and reconciliation, as much more of our indigenous history has come to light. How do we find the goodness of God in this? We live in a moment that can change history forever. Firstly, we must call evil what it is—evil. The atrocities that happened, many in the name of religion, were *not* from the real Jesus. The real Jesus set me free in that tent meeting and continues to walk with me daily. He is good, and He gives us the power to forgive the unforgiveable and love the unlovable. As we grow in His goodness, love, and peace, we can be a light to others in the healing process. We stand together in faith in God's ability to help us do what we can't do ourselves. Walking as one, we can prepare the way for restoration, reconciliation, and revival.

Jesus, I thank you for reaching down into my dark moments and reminding me that you're still there. Strengthen my resolve to forgive and give fresh starts to others. In your name I ask. Amen.

A Rare King

*… Out of the virtue stored in their hearts, good and up-
right people will produce good fruit … For the overflow
of what has been stored in your heart will be seen by your
fruit and will be heard in your words.* (Luke 6:45, TPT)

Can you imagine being appointed king at the age of eight? That's
when Josiah, one of the world's youngest kings, began his reign.
Scripture records Josiah as a godly king who came to the throne following the assassination of his father, King Amon. He ruled as the King
of Judah from approximately 640 to 609 B.C. Second Kings 22:2 introduces Josiah by saying, *"And he did what was right in the eyes of the
Lord … he did not turn aside to the right hand or to the left"* (NKJV). I
love this exemplary description of Josiah's life. If this were all the Bible
told us about him, that would be impressive enough, but we also learn
that from start to finish, he never failed in his right living and his passion
to point his people back to God.

He raised money to repair the temple, and during the repairs, the
high priest found the Book of the Law. When it was read to Josiah, he
tore his clothes in mourning and repentance. After fifty-seven years of
massive idolatry (under Manasseh, his grandfather, and Amon, his father), during which God was ignored and His goodness trampled on,
Josiah knew that there must be change (2 Kings 22:10–11). *"And the
king stood by the pillar and made a covenant before the Lord, to walk after
the Lord and to keep his commandments and his testimonies … And all the
people joined in the covenant"* (2 Kings 23:3, ESV).

His repentance wasn't simply lip service. He removed the articles of
worship to pagan Gods and had them burned. He removed the idola-

trous priests and burned the Asherah poles. He tore down the housing of the shrine prostitutes. His place of influence gave opportunity to turn a nation back to God. It's easy to see why Josiah was identified as a "good" king. Every decision he made flowed out of a heart of obedience to God. What an encouraging report! *"Neither before nor after Josiah was there a king like him who turned to the Lord as he did- with all his heart and with all his soul and with all his strength ..."* (2 Kings 23:25a).

As I consider his life, his choices, and the example he set, I'm encouraged to take stock of my own life. What's my response when confronted with the truth of God's Word? Are there idols residing in this temple of the Holy Spirit? Do I still weep and repent over sin, or do I look for excuses to stay comfortable in it? As I look at Josiah, am I reminded that the circumstances of my life and upbringing don't define me, but my response to God does? Am I fully committed to do what is right in God's eyes? Am I displaying the character of the good God whom I serve?

The Holy Spirit helps us to identify areas in our lives where change is needed. I am choosing to ask myself these hard questions and respond in a way that will keep me on track to finish well, bringing glory to Him. Perhaps you could use this opportunity today to do the same.

Father, may it be said of me that I did right in the eyes of the Lord. Show me how to build character and grow in goodness as I take stock today, even if it hurts. I worship you, and you alone. In Jesus' name.

Busted

Day Twelve

Contributed by Sherry Stahl

For you were once darkness, but now you are light in the Lord. Live as children of light (for the fruit of the light consists in all goodness, righteousness and truth) (Ephesians 5:8–9)

We were having fun. There were about seventy-five adults and teenagers at long, sprawling tables, eating lunch in the church meeting hall after the Sunday morning service before play practice started. A lady I'd never seen before leaned out and pointed at me. She emphatically said in a voice loud enough to be heard over the chatter, "You must be John Fletcher's daughter!"

Maureen came over and explained that she'd grown up with my dad, and she told everyone that my loud voice and talkative nature was just like him. Busted. We Fletchers have never been known to be quiet people, and I have definitely not veered far from family genetics in that respect. Talking a lot, what used to get me in trouble at school and during play practices, is now what people pay me to do. Funny, isn't it.

In Ephesians 5, Paul first talks about how believers should be imitators of God. He continues in that same train of thought and begins explaining that believers are children of light. Verses 8–9 have given me a lot to think about, and I hope you'll give them a second thought too.

If you've come to faith in Christ, then you are now light in the Lord. Christ shines through you. Verse 9 makes the expectation even clearer when Paul says you're to *"live as children of light,"* not fourth cousins half-removed. No, you're called to live as children of light, and children have undeniable, unmistakable, unconcealable traits of their parents.

Like my issues with sometimes talking too much, each child will have distinctive characteristics that reveal who their parents are.

As believers, the character traits of our Father should be so evident that it's clear to the people around us who we belong to. The more time we spend with Daddy, the more like Him we should become. If God is the light, and through Christ we become the light and are expected to live like the light, then we better make sure we know how the light behaves.

Jesus demonstrated God's nature in every way: *"He is the radiance of the glory of God and the exact imprint of his nature …"* (Hebrews 1:3a, ESV). First Chronicles 16:34 and Psalm 107:1 both say, *"Give thanks to the Lord, for he is good; his love endures forever."* Nahum 1:7 tells us that *"The Lord is good, a stronghold in the day of trouble, and He knows those who take refuge in Him"* (NASB).

God is good. It's His nature, and out of that nature flows goodness. His Word reveals that He has an abundance of goodness stored up for those who fear Him and take refuge in Him (Psalm 31:19).

It's important to make sure that the fruit of goodness is abundantly on display in your life, pointing people toward the Father of lights in an undeniable, unmistakable, unconcealable way, so that someone could point a finger at you and emphatically say, "You must be a Christian!"

Jesus, may it be unmistakeable to the people around me who I belong to. May my light shine brighter as I spend more time with you. Thank you for the abundance of goodness you have stored up for me so that I can change circumstances and atmospheres for those who need your goodness. Amen.

Think about This ...

Day Thirteen
Contributed by Jennifer Vaughan Hay

*... Fix your thoughts on what is true and good and right.
Think about things that are pure and lovely, and dwell on
the fine, good things in others. Think about all you can
praise God for and be glad about.* (Philippians 4:8, TLB)

I love this verse. It's full of truth, hope, and good instruction. It reminds
me that God's good gifts should be viewed as blessings that lead us
back to Him. When our eyes look beyond the natural to the beautiful
blessings of God and His goodness, we will ultimately come to a place
of praise and gratitude.

I have a sweet and caring friend who is raising a son living with
Down Syndrome. She once told me that she viewed her son's condition
as a gift, and I was taken aback. Seeing the long list of medical appointments, the delayed milestones, and an uncertain future, I wondered if
she really meant a gift. As I leaned in to understand more, she readily
unpacked her assessment with genuine certainty. She wasn't in denial,
nor did she minimize the struggles, but she had grown to understand
something beyond the natural.

She taught me that every individual is unique, and her child's
uniqueness is a precious blessing. Her son's presence has taught her family patience, compassion, and the incredible strength of love. She cher-
ishes each milestone, no matter how small, and celebrates the beauty in
his differences. He has brought immeasurable joy into her life, reminding her daily of the simple yet profound truth that God's love knows no
bounds. She's grateful for this extraordinary gift from God, for it has
enriched her life in ways she never could have imagined.

Recently I changed jobs. It was a change I believed God was calling me to. As an act of obedience, I stepped out of my comfort zone into a larger and more challenging role. During my first few weeks, I was a mess! I felt out of my league, unsettled, inadequate. Everything I was used to was different. I needed to get to know new people and establish myself as the new "boss." I was questioning what I had agreed to and was even feeling remorseful. I didn't see this change as a gift, that's for sure.

One teary drive home, the Lord reminded me about my friend and the challenges she faces. I thought about how she lives a life of thanksgiving, even in the hard and unsure times. With her example to follow, I got to work. I dug into my scriptures, worshipped from a deep place within, and spent a lot of time in prayer. *By repositioning my heart to receive this new challenge as a good gift from my Heavenly Father,* I was able to look beyond my feelings and find the strength to persevere. I could see what was lovely and true and pure in both the position and the ministry. I could praise Him for what had seemed like impossible challenges.

Choosing to see each challenge as a gift from our Sovereign Father opens our hearts to receive everything that comes with that gift—patience, unconditional love, grace, strength, a yearning for dependence on Him, and so much more. God never wastes an opportunity to mold our hearts into a closer version of His character. He is the light in the darkness. He is the very definition of goodness and perfection. He is unchanging. Today, with a grateful heart, I fix my thoughts on Him, for He is good and worthy to be praised.

Lord Jesus, today I am choosing to fix my thoughts on what is true and good and right. I bring to the cross my worries, anger, ungodly thoughts, and the lies I have believed about you. Cleanse my heart and mind and help me to walk in love and integrity, displaying your goodness. In your name I ask. Amen.

I See It Now

God, everyone sees your goodness, for your tender love is blended into everything you do. (Psalm 145:9, TPT)

When life is challenging and painful, where is God and His goodness? Fanny Crosby (1820–1915) was blinded at six weeks of age through improper medical treatment of an eye infection. That same year, her father died, leaving her in the care of her twenty-one-year-old mother and her maternal grandmother. The struggling family moved to New York within a few years.

Determined that her granddaughter would flourish despite blindness, Grandma Eunice read the classics to Fanny and led her through the memorization of numerous scripture passages. Fanny's incredible memory and her constant intake of scripture reportedly saw her able to quote the first four books of both the Old and New Testaments by the age of ten!

When Fanny was fourteen, some total strangers paid for her education at the New York Institution for the Blind. It was a single act of generosity with far-reaching, life-changing consequence. After seven years of education, Fanny graduated from the Institute but remained for eleven more years as a member of the teaching staff.

The truths of God's Word eventually came alive to Fanny after attendance at a revival meeting, where she accepted Christ and began her personal relationship with God. Though Fanny could have been bitter and resentful, she didn't let her physical disability stop her from praising God and sharing His goodness and love with others.

When Fanny was thirty-eight years old, she married a fellow teacher and gifted organist from the New York Institute for the Blind, Alexander Van Alstyne. Their only child, a daughter Frances, died in her sleep shortly after birth, a great and devastating loss.

After many years of mourning, Fanny said she had finally found her purpose, and she began to compose hymns and poems full of passionate gratefulness to God. She provided the church with some of its best loved hymns, eventually writing approximately nine thousand hymns under a variety of pen names. When she was not writing songs, she was expressing God's goodness through working in churches and missions, nursing the sick, and caring for the poor.

"I am shut out of the world and shut in with my Lord. The Lord is the sunshine of my soul. To God be the glory!"[1]

I love the third stanza from her hymn "Blessed Assurance":

> Perfect submission, all is at rest,
> I in my Savior am happy and blest;
> Watching and waiting, looking above,
> *Filled with His goodness, lost in His love.*
> This is my story, this is my song,
> Praising my Savior all the day long.[2]

If you feel you've been blindsided by life's circumstances, or God's answer to your prayers doesn't seem imminent, look for His goodness. "To weep and sigh because I'm blind? I cannot and I won't."[3] May Fanny's life encourage you to let the praising begin.

Heavenly Father, your solutions are far better than I could conceive. I'm choosing today to trust you when I can't see what's ahead. Amen.

[1] "Fanny J. Crosby on Faith: 7 Quotes in 7 Days," Living by Design Ministries, accessed December 7, 2023, https://livingbydesign.org/fanny-crosby-on-faith-7-quotes-in-7-days/.

[2] Fanny J. Crosby (1873), "Blessed Assurance," Hymnary.org, https://hymnary.org/text/blessed_assurance_jesus_is_mine.

[3] "Fanny Crosby," Quotefancy, accessed December 7, 2023, https://quotefancy.com/quote/1621432/.

Stranded in the Mountains

Day Fifteen
Contributed by Julie Stautland

*I remain confident of this: I will see the goodness of the
Lord in the land of the living.* (Psalm 27:13)

Sitting on the side of the road was becoming a familiar experience. Our dark blue Ford maxi van, which we lovingly nicknamed "Fix or repair daily" or "Found on roadside dead," had a habit of developing one or two issues a week. Anyone with financial means would have either drained their wallet to repair it completely or directed it to the local junkyard. As four itinerant actors of a Christian ministry, we didn't have the luxury of either one. We were really "living on a prayer."

One scorching and humid Sunday afternoon, we were driving through the mountains of West Virginia. We had performed in a morning service and had just enough time to make it to our evening church location. When our van suddenly sputtered to a stop and died in the middle of the mountains, we moved into strategy-and-survival mode. This was before cell phones, but my fiancé often communicated to truckers on a CB radio. As he put out a call for help, the rest of us prayed for a miracle.

We were curious about how our good and faithful God would work in this situation. We fluctuated between faith and the distress of the outcome if we missed the performance. The donation income we expected to receive would provide us with gas for the next week, our host home accommodations, and food. So we sat and prayed and tried to find shade and cool.

We had learned from living on the road that we needed to depend on God to move the hearts of people we met along the way. None of us were from West Virginia. But there was one person out of all of our travels on this trip who came to mind. Though our interactions with him had been brief, his character, kindness, and generosity exemplified the goodness of God. Mr. Smiley!

A passing trucker was kind enough to stop and take my fiancé to a pay phone at the nearest gas station. He made a call to Mr. Smiley, who had accommodated us a couple of weeks earlier. Without hesitation, he drove one and a half hours to pick us up on the side of the highway. He continued driving us all the way to our next church, even further from his own home, so we could make it in time to minister.

The next day, he made the long drive back to us with his pickup truck. He towed our sad-looking van from the side of the mountain highway back to a garage in his town. Although that was far more gracious than we could have imagined, he blessed us extravagantly by paying the total bill for the repairs.

Mr. Smiley was not a rich man. He and his wife had experienced profound pain throughout their lives, but he remained faithful to God and chose to love freely. He sacrificed his time and money for people he barely knew. We had no money or gift to give him, just our gratitude.

For years we spoke about the incredible kindness of this West Virginia-based good Samaritan and how it impacted our personal walks with Jesus. Beyond his own problems, he chose to smile and show God's love to those in need. He was a "good" man who walked in the fruit of the Spirit—sacrificial love, patience, kindness, faithfulness—and he truly lived up to his name: Mr. Smiley.

Lord, I want to be an extravagant blesser who displays your goodness in unexpected ways. You have given me so much that I can share. Ready my heart for your next invitation. In Jesus' name. Amen.

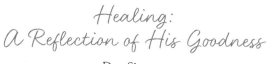

Healing:
A Reflection of His Goodness

Day Sixteen

Oh, that men would give thanks to the Lord for His goodness, And for His wonderful works to the children of men!
(Psalm 107:8, NKJV)

The New Testament records many eyewitness accounts of Jesus' time on earth, showing goodness to everyone He met. Since He is like the Father in every way, we have faith-building accounts of how His words and actions brought healing, hope, and life.

In Matthew's Gospel, we read that "… *people soon began bringing to him all who were sick. And whatever their sickness or disease, or if they were demon possessed or epileptic or paralyzed—he healed them <u>all</u>*" (Matt 4:24b, NLT, emphasis added). In a world full of pain, disease, injustice, and confusion, Jesus brought goodness. Think of the leper He cleansed, or the man lowered through a hole in a roof. Both were healed and forgiven. Even a dead girl was brought to life. Those He touched experienced His goodness. Today His goodness works to bring change in our mindsets, situations, and actions, as His life-giving power is still at work.

When I think back to my childhood, I find my place alongside the healed and grateful. As a five-year-old, just before elementary school, I was enticed from the yard of my home by a "nice" man who was taking me to the circus. I'll simply say that there was no circus, the man wasn't nice, and there was only evil and darkness. But the works of the enemy were interrupted by an unexpected rainstorm that allowed me to find a way of escape. I know that my promptings and courage, at such a young age, were gifts of Divine intervention. Psalm 18:9,11b, 17 says: "*He opened the heavens and came down … veiling his approach with dark rain clouds. He rescued me from my powerful enemies, from those who ... were too strong for me"* (NLT). He rescued me because He delighted in me, and I mattered to Him. That's a good God!

The perpetrator's charges and sentencing brought a minimal level of closure as I began school with a dark cloud surrounding me. Joy was surface deep because, for me, people were scary and not to be trusted. I needed God's goodness to intervene in my anxious and fearful mind.

As soon as I learned to read, my Bible became a lifeline. The Lord showed me that His plan was to *"Let light shine out of darkness"* (2 Corinthians 4:6). With the light of His truth, a powerful healing began. Allowing Him to fill my life with truth upon truth gave me the strength I needed as a young teenager to evict fear and shame and to forgive. While counselling and conversation were unavailable, He sent His Word to heal and restore. As I spent time with Him, I began to "know" Him. He was faithful, honest, kind, and safe. I was able to forgive not only the perpetrator but everyone who unknowingly contributed to my darkness. My forgiveness didn't erase the memory or change the event. It had nothing to do with absolving the criminal of his crime. But my act of forgiveness broke the power of the wrongdoer and the event over me! Fear left, and peace came. *I share this because it is a story of good news!*

His goodness was reflected in every part of the journey, and today I live free of any attached pain or fear. Jesus came to set captives free, to heal the sick and bring light in the darkness, and He hasn't changed. Perhaps you need to believe this truth for someone you know or love. Let's agree in prayer for the miracle of His goodness to step into their impossible situation today.

Lord Jesus, step into my impossible situation today in the way that you know will bring freedom and healing. Show me once again the power of forgiveness. You never change—you are always good. Amen.

A Good Samaritan

Day Seventeen

Our Scriptures tell us that if you see your enemy hungry,
go buy that person lunch, or if he's thirsty, get him a drink.
Your generosity will surprise him with goodness. Don't let
evil get the best of you; get the best of evil by doing good.
(Romans 12:20–21, MSG)

How many times a day or week do you hear the expression, "That person was being a Good Samaritan"? It's common to hear it in the regular evening "good news" stories. It stands out as a great headline; it's the kind of report that makes communities proud.

In the parable of the Good Samaritan, Jesus, however, paints a picture that makes it very clear how to respond to the needs that come our way. He tells the story in response to an expert in the law who demanded clarification on who should be considered a neighbour (Luke 10:25–37).

The parable goes as follows. A man going from Jerusalem to Jericho was attacked by robbers along the way, who left him badly beaten and stripped of his clothes. Three different travellers came upon this helpless victim, and each had his own response. The priest crossed to the other side of the road, relinquishing any responsibility to help. The Levite counted the risk and did the same. But the Samaritan (viewed by Jews as inferior and even repulsive) immediately felt compassion for the man, bandaged his wounds, and took him to a nearby inn, paying for his care and recovery. Jesus asked the lawyer which one of these he would consider a neighbour. The clever lawyer was cornered—he must, of course, choose the one who had shown goodness and compassion. Jesus then directed him to go and do the same.

If we're going to grow in this fruit of the Spirit, we must be willing to leave our personal comfort zones and put our convictions into action. Sadly, we miss many opportunities to share God's goodness. The priest and the Levite asked themselves, "If I stop to help this man, what will happen to me?" But the Samaritan asked, "If I fail to stop to help this man, what will happen to him?" I think God wants us to see what comes our way as His invitation to be Christlike, not simply an inconvenience. When Jesus saw people in need, their status, their past, their gender, their disease, or their wealth didn't matter.

I recall one very snowy Sunday afternoon on our way home from church when we came across a poorly dressed middle-aged man who had fallen trying to cross the street. While he struggled to right himself, he fell again, and the blood on his face stood stark against the white snow. His coat had come loose and lay beside him. His situation was clearly dangerous. We heard a mix of incoherent and foul language as we pulled over to help. I had grown up watching my mother help many men in similar situations, so I knew I should go. It was a compliant but messy rescue, and the back seat of the car told the tale. Some friends who happened by warned me of the risky diseases we might contract from assisting him.

God in His goodness had provided us with everything this man needed, including His love. If we failed to stop, what could have happened to him? It was God's invitation to do good. And that's what mattered.

No human law will compel you to cross over to the person in that ditch or step into that struggle that you'll meet later this week. But if you do—if you choose to move toward the pain of others rather than around it—you'll be walking the way of Jesus. You will offer a little taste of God's goodness that they won't forget.

Lord, I confess that I'm not always agreeable when I'm inconvenienced. I'm grateful for your goodness, and I open my heart to your invitations to show mercy and kindness, even when I least expect it. Amen.

Wrapped in His Goodness
Day Eighteen

He forgives your sins ... He crowns you with love and mercy
... He wraps you in goodness ... He renews your youth—
you're always young in his presence. (Psalm 103:3–5, MSG)

As a mom, grandmother, and previous teacher, children haven't been far from my sight. One of the things I love best about them is their ruthless honesty. Spunky, curious risktaker would describe my grandson Joshua as he set out to begin school. I'm not sure much has changed now that he's heading into his twenties, driving his car, dating, and graduating from college.

Joshua and his siblings grew up only a few miles down the road from us, so we spent lots of time together. He never ran out of unanswerable questions, and he believed he could do anything—consequences and actions seemed rather detached. Injuries were common, as he was sure that with the right equipment, the right super cape, and the right ledge, he could fly. Failure and temporary immobility weren't a deterrent to try again. As well, he always hoped to make some great discoveries by dismantling ordinary objects and putting them back together. His teachers regularly disciplined him for "ruining" classroom items while he was "inventing." He had to get to the bottom of what made things tick.

When Joshua asked Jesus to be his friend and Saviour at age four, it was no different. A few weeks after his decision, while babysitting the children, I helped him with prayers, read him his favourite book, and tucked him in for sleep. Not many minutes later, I heard the bedsheets rustling and found Joshua under the mess of covers near the bottom of his bed. I was puzzled about whether he had brought a frog to bed, was having a bad dream, or experiencing a medical issue. When I was able to get him back to the pillow, he explained his dilemma. Since he had asked Jesus into his heart, he was bending his head to his chest in various contortions, trying to find Him. He wanted Him to come out to talk. Following a short lesson on prayer, Joshua's absolutely sincere conversation with God that followed was precious. He thanked me and reported he could now "feel Him in there."

Children seem innocently able to express their authentic feelings and experiences of God and to God, which we, as adults, can often suppress, minimize, or ignore. When we can't see God's goodness in our situations, or don't see the answers to prayer that we expect, we may deeply feel that God isn't dependable, that He doesn't care, that our relationship with Him is conditional, or that the God we worship in church isn't One we can experience in everyday life. And sometimes we stop searching and leave the conversation.

While we hold in tension the reality of our wounds, losses, and the injustices of our broken world, the truth is that for believers, God's character is goodness, and there is a challenging call for us to trust Him when it seems we can't find Him. This isn't easy, but I believe that it's required of us in order to engage in the greatest gift we have been offered—a personal relationship with a good God.

Conversations with God, whether they're laments or praise, simplistic or profound, bring us that greater sense of His presence that we otherwise fail to grasp. We are wrapped in His goodness. I love what John Ortberg said: "Prayer becomes real when we grasp the reality and goodness of God's constant presence with 'the real me.'"[4] May we revisit the joy of knowing His presence is with "the real me" and "the childlike, searching me" in every situation of our day.

Lord, I want to be able to express my authentic feelings and experiences to you. You already know them! I know you want even the questions of my heart. I'm coming closer today to be wrapped in your presence. Thank you for your open arms. Amen.

---

[4] "John Ortberg," AZquotes, accessed December 8, 2023, https://www.azquotes.com/quote/403602?ref=goodness-of-god.

The Struggle

Day Nineteen

I know that in me, that is, in my fallen human nature, there is nothing good. I can will myself to do something good, but that does not help me carry it out. I can determine that I am going to do good, but I don't do it; instead, I end up living out the evil that I decided not to do. (Romans 7:18–19, VOICE)

Do you ever find yourself spending time and energy trying to convince others that you're something you know you're not—that you're kind, confident, skilled, or good-hearted when you know you don't really believe it yourself?

John Corcoran knows what it's like to "cover-up" or fail to do the very thing he wanted to do. He never learned to read or write, and he was a troublemaker in elementary school. Exhausted teachers kept promoting him to the next grade. In high school, he mastered new skills when he started cheating by turning in other peoples' papers as his own. He could read the system and people.

He cheated his way through Texas Western, graduating with a degree in education! As a teacher, he taught in high school for seventeen years, using two or three teacher's assistants in each class to do board work or read the bulletin. While John likely began with good motives, the pretending became comfortable and normal. I can't imagine the constant inner *fear* of being found out and the *shame* of not being able or willing to turn things around. Leaving teaching to become a real estate developer necessitated his learning to read and write. John attended a small Literary Centre where a senior lady tutored him through to grade six level. He later became an advocate for better educational systems.[5]

I suspect we've all experienced varying degrees of wishing and hoping, sometimes even pretending. We can live trying to persuade ourselves, others, and God Himself that we're "good" people. But deep inside, we question the truth of such an assessment. It is in that awareness that we understand the struggle Paul shares in Romans 7:18–25.

Based on his many letters and his influence for the gospel, we might describe Paul as the uncommon Apostle—a blessed and transformed man, an ambassador of Christ who suffered much for God, a favourite of heaven, a spiritual father of thousands! But he sees himself as a wretched man who hadn't met the mark. He failed to do the good he wanted to do and instead did the very things he despised. He was, like us, one great collection of contradictions.

There can be no progress in cultivating righteous living until we learn what Paul learned here—that in me (that is, in my flesh) lives nothing good. The flesh here means the evil, corrupt nature. We simply don't have the resources to translate desire into action. But in verse 25a, Paul gives us the good news: *"I am thankful to God for the freedom that comes through our Lord Jesus, the Anointed One!"* (VOICE). *That's it right there.* Our hope to function out of our new nature and carry His presence resides in our surrender. We walk in His righteousness, not our own (2 Corinthians 5:21).

Paul became one of the most influential apostles, spreading the gospel throughout the world. God's grace can transform anyone. In the light of our own inadequacies and struggles, we, too, receive redemption, significance, and freedom through surrender to Jesus, the Anointed and Righteous One.

God, I sometimes feel the weariness in hiding the truth. I ask forgiveness and welcome your presence. Surrendered to you, I see victory!

---

[5] Charisse Yu, "Retired Teacher Reveals He Was Illiterate Until Age 48," *San Diego News*, February 14, 2008, https://faculty.tamucc.edu/dcrumbley/Crumbley%20Homepage/illiterate-teacher-until-age-48.pdf.

The Overwhelming Goodness of God

Day Twenty
Contributed by Amenla Cunningham

Oh, how great is Your goodness,
Which You have laid up for those who fear You,
Which You have prepared for those who trust in You
In the presence of the sons of men!
(Psalm 31:19, NKJV)

True goodness is the declaration of Christlikeness in the believer's life. Goodness partners with other fruit of the Spirit in our lives as an expression of God's relentless love. As we experience God's goodness through others, it resonates in our bones, and we long to articulate this goodness in our own actions and responses.

From a young age, I understood I was required to do good, but I often did the opposite. I constantly struggled to overcome evil with good. My flesh struggled to follow the rules. The enemy of my soul often filled my mind with negative thoughts that brought confusion instead of victory, but praise God, that isn't the end of the story!

A little more than four decades ago, a massive wave of revival broke out in a village in Nagaland, in Northeast India. Our family lived in a neighbouring village. During this revival, my mother, a single mother of eight children, encountered God in a way she'd never anticipated. This began a new and exciting walk with Jesus as provider, healer, promise-keeper, and often miracle-worker. My greatest surprise was that God could not only transform mothers, but He knew my name and welcomed me into a personal journey with Him. As a ten-year-old, when God's presence touched me during that revival, my mind and heart were transformed by His love. Though our circumstances remained the same, we saw our situation through a new lens, awakened to God's goodness even in the struggles.

As I entered young adulthood, my simple prayer and heart's desire was to find a husband whose priority would be to love God and then also me. What a surprise when God used my obedience to Him during Bible school to drop me right into His perfect plan for a soulmate and ministry partner. God had opened my heart to cross-cultural missions—how wise is our God! I didn't realize that my man of God's heart was being touched in a similar way. God was about to bring together two very different cultures from India and make them life partners and pastors.

God has surrounded us with opportunities to step into many lives in their moments of crisis, and we can only marvel at the miracles of transformation. Since 2015, we've been blessed to provide a safe place for restoration of dignity and destiny for children rescued from sex trafficking. The goodness of God has provided staff, each one uniquely gifted in distributing His love, who are implementing education and giving food, shelter, medical care, and nurture within a vibrant, faith-based environment.

On a personal level, we've been blessed with a son, a recently married daughter, and a great son-in-law, all of whom love Jesus. Sometimes we can't fathom the depth of His love and goodness. Dearly beloved, I pray that as you read this devotion, you experience the goodness of God! May you see how God's goodness can penetrate evil, bringing hope and freedom. May you keep in step with the Holy Spirit so that others may taste of His goodness through you.

O Lord, how great is your goodness. I worship you. All that I am or ever hope to be is found in you. You are my redeemer, provider, guide, and salvation. May I live out a vibrant testimony of your goodness to a hurting world. In Jesus' name. Amen.

A More Excellent Way

"The thing which you have said to do is good." (Deuteronomy 1:14b, NASB)

One of the most challenging aspects of being a Christian is accepting the need for change. No one likes to be told that they need to change, but when we see the potential for improvement and greater impact, it becomes somewhat easier to embrace. The Christian life is a continual series of changes (Romans 12:2). We mature in Christ (2 Peter 3:18), and maturity necessitates change. Without such growth and maturing, we can easily fall into error or complacency.

One such opportunity to change is described in Acts 18. Two Jewish Christians, Priscilla and Aquila, were living in Corinth, where they had set up their tentmaking business. Priscilla and Aquila opened their home to Paul and invited him to work with them. He invested in their lives, teaching them the ways of the Lord. Priscilla and Aquila grew and matured in the faith so much that, a year later, he entrusted them to start the work in Ephesus without him.

While they were caring for the Ephesian church, a passionate Jewish believer named Apollos came to town (Acts 18:24–26). He was a skilled orator and knew the scriptures well. But there was so much more for him to learn. He knew nothing about the work of the Holy Spirit. Priscilla and Aquila were wise and discerning, and they walked with integrity. They sensed that it would be helpful to take this young preacher aside and explain to Apollos the way of God that was *"more excellent."* He wasn't wrong in what he was teaching, but they helped him take his knowledge of the Lord to the next level. While they also appreciated the gift of excellence in oratory in his life, they helped steward his journey of growth. They walked him through an invitation for change that would help him increase the effectiveness of the gospel. As a passionate lover of God already, I suspect his willingness to adjust came quickly and very likely with great joy and fresh revelation.

Ephesians 1:17–19 reflects the heart of Paul's pastoral prayer for the believers in Ephesus. His desire was for them to embrace change and growth—to grow in wisdom, revelation, and awareness of God's mighty power at work in their lives. These verses serve as a timeless reminder for believers to seek a deeper relationship with God and to experience the transformative power of His Spirit in their daily lives. As we embrace this prayer, we're drawn closer to God's heart and purpose for us, finding strength and assurance in His abundant goodness. It's easy to grow distant in our relationship with Him if we simply stay satisfied with the status quo. As hungry and thirsty ones, however, we, like Apollos, can seize an opportunity to understand the greatness of God that we don't yet know and have not yet experienced.

After twenty-five years as a believer, the apostle Paul said that he had not yet attained to knowing Christ fully, but he pressed on toward that goal (Philippians 3:8–14). And if that was true of Paul, how much more is it true of us! To press on means to prepare for and welcome change. As the prophet Hosea wrote, *"Let us press on to know him"* (Hosea 6:3, NLT).

> *"being confident of this, that he who began a good work in you will carry it on to completion until the day of Christ Jesus"* (Philippians 1:6)

Heavenly Father, thank you for renewing me day by day. I realize that only you can create a real change in me. I embrace those opportunities to grow in the knowledge of a "more excellent way." Thank you for your presence in my life. Being transformed to become more like you is truly a good thing.

Aligning with His Goodness

Day Twenty-Two
Contributed by Meghan VanderKruk

The Lord is good to all, and His tender mercies are over all His works. (Psalm 145:9, NKJV)

Sometimes I get caught up in the vastness of God, and I wonder if He hears or cares for me. In response to these questions, He plants a memory of the first time I felt His closeness, and the many ways He's spoken to me in His still, small voice.

I've recently been drawn to recall the story of Joseph. He was loved by his father and honoured with a special coat but hated by his brothers. He struggled at home, as they mocked him, envied him, and plotted against him. Family is God's idea, and each person has a God-given role. Fathers are meant to protect, provide, and give value/identity. Mothers are meant to nourish, comfort, and guide. Brothers are meant to love and affirm, cherish, and celebrate (Hebrews 13:1; Luke 15:32). But when a relationship is shattered, a painful crisis ensues. God weeps, and the entire family suffers. In Joseph's story, he was a victim of the sin and choices of others. What happened to him was unjust and undeserved.

Being in a place of pain that has come because of the choices of others may be more common than it seems. As a child, youth, or young adult, it can be devastating when the picture you've painted of a parent on a pedestal comes crashing to the ground. For me, in the disappointment and shock, I found myself facing painful emotions, wondering how to move forward. I mourned the loss of something that seemed beautiful. I was overwhelmed and vulnerable.

While I could recite the truths of God's character, I didn't believe that what He had for my future was goodness as promised in Romans

8:28 and Psalm 145:9. My greatest fear was being alone with my emotions because I felt they were too big and would consume me. I was on the brink of burnout from working four jobs, busying myself to create distraction. But God said, "I have goodness for you to experience in this, and goodness for you on the other side."

One day while doing some work at a cafe, I heard a still, small whisper: "I am healing you in the background. I'm doing this because I love you." I immediately broke down. It came at a time when I wasn't begging Him for an answer, but He chose to wrap me up in the comfort of His goodness. He was working on my behalf, even when I was unaware of it. This is who God is. He has such a tender heart for His kids that He will interrupt you in the mundane and breathe encouragement and hope over you. In every step of Joseph's journey, the Lord was with him. (Genesis 39:2), and His whisper was a reminder that He was with me.

He offers an invitation into a space where you'll come face to face with the war within, but there too God resides. A vulnerability that may seem scary, but one that is better than you could imagine. Here, in silence and solitude, He'll reveal the truth that He's a good God and that through an intimate relationship with Him, one can experience healing on this side of heaven.

God authored the greatest love story of all—sending His Son to pave a way for restoration. He offers grace, already knowing we're going to mess up. Our life, though tested by doubts and questions at times, can become a beautiful narrative of God making good of what the enemy meant for destruction. Goodness wins when we choose to step into alignment with the truth of who our Father is. If we allow Him to draw us close, we get to begin again to enjoy "life to the full" and glimpse the completeness that will come as we step into eternity—a place where His presence makes even shadows bow before Him.

Lord, you know my inside fears and fights, and you see my future. Draw me close today and remind me that you have paved a way for restoration. With you, I am victorious. Amen.

Amazing Grace

Day Twenty-Three

For it is by grace you have been saved, through faith—
and this is not from yourselves, it is the gift of God—
(Ephesians 2:8)

I seldom do a funeral for someone with family who are unfamiliar to church where "Amazing Grace" isn't the song of choice. It's requested even by the atheist and agnostic. It can be sung together or shared through a video or recording by a wide variety of artists, from Aretha Franklin, Johnny Cash, or Kelly Clarkson to the Vienna Boys' Choir. Most people are familiar with the words of the song, but they would be hard-pressed to tell you exactly what about grace is so amazing. The Christian life, however, from beginning to end, is a life of extraordinary grace.

Grace is God's undeserved kindness and goodness. His grace is extended to us firstly in salvation, but also in everyday life. We benefit from God's grace in all that we do. It's called "Amazing Grace" because God, in his infinite goodness, treats us far better than we deserve. And He takes care of us when we can't take care of ourselves.

In our journey through life, God watches over us 24/7. His kindness and grace steady our uncertain steps, and the same grace provides *"shade"* in the hot spots (Psalm 121:5). He is our source of help and strength if we're willing to turn to Him. Though each day is uncertain and may seem to hold more than a fair share of disappointment, loss, or pain, we have His promise that He will ultimately work it out for our good and His glory. It's hard to see the good when the clouds surround and darkness moves in. As believers, however, we are reassured in knowing that God is in control—always and forever.

Timothy Paul Jones in his book *Proof* describes God's outrageous grace this way:

> Outrageous grace isn't a favor you can achieve by being good; it's the gift you receive by being God's. Outrageous grace is *God's goodness that comes looking for you when you have nothing to offer in return* ... It's one-way love that calls you into the kingdom not because you've been good but because God has chosen you and made you his own. And now he is chasing you to the ends of the earth to keep you ... God ... declared over you, "I ... chose you. No matter what you say or do, neither my love nor my choice will ever change." That's grace that's truly amazing. (emphasis added)[6]

How do you feel when you pause to consider that you are the object of His affection, and all that He expresses comes from an abundant, God-sized goodness toward you? Perhaps you'll be stirred today to invite the Holy Spirit to help you express God's grace through your own written words or song of praise to God as David did. "*I compose songs on your wonders ... I could write a book full of the details of your greatness ... God is all mercy and grace ... (He) is rich in love ... good to one and all; everything he does is soaked through with grace*" Psalm 145:5b–9, MSG).

Take time to respond today as the Holy Spirit leads you.

I am so aware today, Father, that your goodness comes looking for me when I have nothing to offer in return but obedience. Thank you for choosing me and for loving me no matter what. Amen.

---

[6] Daniel Montgomery and Timothy Paul Jones, *Proof* (Grand Rapids, MI: Zondervan, 2014), 82–84.

Up Close and Amazed

Day Twenty-Four

Contributed by Cherie Martin

... God anointed Jesus of Nazareth with the Holy Spirit and with power. He went about doing good and healing all who were oppressed ... for God was with Him. (Acts 10:38, ESV)

Recently I was honoured at a celebration of my twenty-five years as a Registered Nurse at the Hospital for Sick Children in Toronto. I am so blessed to have worked here with this team and these incredible families and children. I often talk about "the highlights" of life and celebrate the little things. When you view the landscape of people's lives, which I see as a nurse, you can't help but *not* sweat the small stuff and see *good* and *God* in everything.

This celebration caused me to reflect. I remember vividly the cherished moments when the call was placed within my heart. As a fourteen-year-old teen babysitting for a missionary family from our church, I remember rocking their little boy late at night. He was fighting leukaemia. I won't ever forget his little, warm body, his tears, and his little bald head tucked under my chin as I cuddled him. I fell in love. I knew in that moment that my desire for the future was to be a paediatric oncology nurse.

My educational path had a few detours, but God knew and worked out my training perfectly. When I graduated, I had just the right experiences to be offered a bone marrow transplant position at Sick Kids. Wow—that was an unlikely spot for a new graduate! God is good! My steps were truly ordered by Him.

My plan was to commute to Toronto for two years to gain experience at this world-renowned hospital, but I'm still here! People laugh and remind me that there are hospitals closer to home. But I'm a Sick Kids "lifer." These kids have my heart, not to mention the extra-ordinary team I get to work with each day! I see God's goodness in my workplace everywhere.

I can't change the diagnosis or the circumstances for my patients, but I can brighten their day in some way. God shows me how to anticipate their needs, and He gives me empathy, kindness, and love for those in my care. He gives me the right words to say when courage is needed, and the energy to go the extra mile to serve those in a time of need. God is a God of love, and miracles still happen! I can pray for my patients and their families through an internal dialogue with God that they know nothing about. Because I carry His presence, even the atmosphere can change! I get to release hope and healing. God gives me His comfort to share in scary situations far beyond my control. I pray before I enter the hospital each shift: "God, it's you and me. We're a team. I'm thankful you never leave me. I am never alone. You are such a good, good God. Please release healing as I care for my patients today." My husband reminds me that as I lean into God and grow in His goodness, even my colleagues benefit from the overflow.

Jesus went about doing good and healing all who were oppressed. As a disciple of Jesus, you are anointed to do His work. You are his hands and feet to help those around you. You can bring light into their darkness and hope into their discouragement. You can speak peace into their storms.

My twenty-five-year celebration is a testimony of His faithfulness in my life. I pray that you will express gratitude for God's goodness in all the little and big things every day. In all that we do, may we always represent who He is—Goodness itself.

Jesus, you have anointed me to carry your hope, comfort, love, and goodness right where you have placed me. Every situation matters to you. Thank you for entrusting me to carry your light. Amen.

Rescued by Goodness

Day Twenty-Five

… do you despise the riches of his goodness, forbearance, and patience, not knowing that the goodness of God leads you to repentance? (Romans 2:4, WEB)

It was just a routine but always unpredictable Wednesday night. Carl picked up some donuts, Kay baked some of her mouth-watering banana cake, and the coffee urns were filled and ready. Next came the heavy lifting as the outreach team tackled the job of moving the most recently donated furniture and the clothing racks to make space for the Bible study.

Since this Salvation Army Thrift Store in Niagara Falls was only a block from the local hospital, we could look forward to welcoming a number of patients from the mental health ward who had earned a pass for the evening. We were never sure who would show up. That Main and Ferry corner was busy and its sidewalks well-trodden, but for all the wrong reasons. Scantily-clothed workers were plentiful, as were their clients. The strip club music reverberated from across the street. But an open door and the offer of hot coffee and treats spread quickly, and by the eighth week, we had some regulars. It wasn't unusual to see twenty to twenty-five sharing seats on the tattered, time-worn couches and the assortment of unique chairs and loveseats.

A new older couple showed up that Wednesday night—clearly not two who would frequent the area. Their eyes and demeanour spoke pain and resistance, but it wasn't long until they engaged in the discussion. Tonight's study was the parable of the lost sheep:

Suppose one of you had a hundred sheep and lost one. Wouldn't you leave the ninety-nine in the wilderness and go after the lost one until you found it? When found, you can be sure you would put it across your shoulders, rejoicing, and when you got home call in your friends and neighbors, saying, "Celebrate with me! I've found my lost sheep!" … there's more joy in heaven over one sinner's rescued life than over ninety-nine good people in no need of rescue. (Luke 15:4–7, MSG)

Ample opportunity was given for the participants in the study to give their interpretation of the parable and find themselves in the story. There was clearly a revelation of the goodness of our Heavenly Father for many in that room, probably for the very first time. Some decided that night to let Him rescue them. Among those who received salvation were the new couple, Marion and Jake.

It was the first night of many more for Marion and Jake, who became regulars and started to help with the coffee and cake. A few weeks went by before Marion shared her story about the night she met Jesus. She and Jake were on their way to the falls. She had decided to end her life. The loss of two children, the lifestyle of crime and repeated incarceration of another, addiction in the family, and the uncertainty of health had all become too much to bear. But God! They realized that the Shepherd we had talked about had reached out His rod and staff and drawn them into that messy, crowded, sweaty thrift store. They mattered to Him.

As they grew to understand God's goodness in new ways, they allowed the Holy Spirit to grow the fruit of goodness in their lives, sharing that goodness with others simply by making themselves available to serve.

God goes to great lengths to rescue us. If you ever find yourself lost, remember that His goodness is chasing you down. What a faithful God!

Jesus, you are such a good shepherd. I pray for those today who need to come into the fold. I ask that their hearts would be softened and their spiritual ears attuned to your gentle promptings of love. Amen.

The Angel in a Navy Suit

Day Twenty-Six
Contributed by Jan Finochio

For you, O Lord, are good and forgiving, abounding in steadfast love to all who call upon you. (Psalm 86:5, ESV)

As I opened the apartment door, there she was again on the floor. Inebriated. My heart sank. Another day that Mom wouldn't be asking how my school day had been.

Dad was a household name as a singer/actor in our region in the 1950s and 60s. Most of us eight kids were in TV commercials or magazine/newspaper ads regularly for popular brands. It wasn't unusual to be taken out of school for the day for a film or commercial shoot in Toronto. My parents made a lot of money when one of us kids would bring in double a man's weekly wage for just an afternoon's work.

But Dad's heart attack changed everything for us. With relationship issues and financial worries, Mom and Dad split up. After a major operation, Mom suffered from phantom pain and found herself on painkillers and meds for depression. Alcohol became her constant friend.

There were still five children at home to raise when Mom was left alone. On her meagre mother's allowance, she struggled to provide for our needs. The culture of the 1960s offered us ample opportunity for rebellion and independence, and we jumped on board. Dad was a committed Catholic and sometimes we went to church, but no faith practices carried over to home. Mom had given up on the church, and in her depression, she was blind to the provision that *had* come. As her alcoholism grew worse, she was in and out of the hospital. Dad visited and contributed, but the situation was chaotic at best.

Things began to change for me in September of my eighteenth year. My sister and I were in downtown Hamilton, busking in front of Jackson Square Mall. Using our skills as folk artists, we could make enough gas money for our truck. An angel in a three-piece, navy tailored suit, working at Eames Men's Wear in that same location, searched for souls on his lunch hour. He invited us to a Bible study, took our contact information, and followed up with a phone call. I responded to the invite with a yes. That night in an old storefront on York Blvd., I found myself praying and inviting Jesus into my life: *"Behold, I stand at the door and knock: if any man hear my voice … I will come in to him, and will sup with him, and he with me"* (Revelation 3:20, KJV).

What a new beginning! What a fresh start! That prayer changed *everything.* I met goodness, peace, and hope that night. His name was Jesus. I don't remember the content of the study, but that navy-suited angel (Michael) read a passage in John 3 with me, where Jesus talked about us being born again, and the Holy Spirit revealed truth. I was aware of my pain, my sin, and my need for God's help. Forgiving others, especially my mom, would be hard, but I knew that because of God's forgiveness toward me, the old things had gone, and all things were becoming new (2 Corinthians 5:17).

Now armed with Jesus, I felt able to go back into the fight. I knew I wasn't alone. What an incredible opportunity for change had been presented. Although circumstances at home remained challenging, I had changed. Light was dispelling darkness, and I could visualize a clearer path forward. I had hope and a future that was in His hands. He has not let me down. Today, I still depend on His help. He is true to His Word: *"I am the light of the world: he that followeth me shall not walk in darkness, but shall have the light of life"* (John 8:12, KJV).

Heavenly Father, it seems we need Michaels today more than ever. Stir my heart so that I abound in love. I want to share your goodness and hope with those who need to meet you. Amen.

Goodness and Light

Day Twenty-Seven

In the same way, let your light shine before others, that they may see your good deeds and glorify your Father in heaven. (Matthew 5:16)

Advent is the time for believers to remember who we are and that we live and move and have our being in the everlasting love that is God Himself. Because of the baby who came at Christmas and brought salvation at the cross, we are hidden in Him. He is the indwelling One, and He is goodness and light.

The season always brings me to review again the importance of the light that came to pierce the darkness, the light that came to bring hope, that true light that speaks goodness and righteousness. Even though we may feel alone, separated, overwhelmed, or lost, Christmas reminds us that we are tucked into His love. Some denominations light the candles of the advent wreath and consider the joy and peace that came with the coming of the Christ child.

My husband and I spent many summers giving oversight to programs at a summer camp on Lake Erie, which for four weeks accommodated underprivileged children from inner cities of Ontario. During the children's camp, we'd have to stay up late, making sure that all counsellors had been able to settle the ten dozen eight-to-twelve-year-olds and attend to any homesickness, sleeplessness, or behavioural issues. Away from the city, in the stillness of the night, we could hear the clicking of the crickets, the lapping of the waves against the shore, and the occasional squeak of a cabin door. Our favourite place to wait through those late evenings was the base of the flagpole. Flashlights were needed to light our way from cabin to cabin, and then we'd return to the raised cement base beneath the flagpole, and we would wait.

On occasional nights, we'd bring a sleeping bag and lay it open on the grass. We'd lie beneath the black velvet of a sky teeming with stars and marvel at God's creation. It was here we saw the northern lights for the first time—flashes of green dancing and parading majestically amidst the stars. On those nights, waiting in that light was truly spiritual.

I could identify a few of the constellations, but I certainly didn't know how to read the sky like the shepherds did on their way to find Jesus, or like the wisemen did in their journey. It's strange how lowly shepherds and wealthy foreigners understood the light and were the first to celebrate His coming, while Herod, the one who was supposed to be the fount of knowledge regarding the Jewish people, was left in the dark.

Throughout the Old Testament, light is regularly associated with God and His Word, with salvation, goodness, truth, and life. Light signifies God's goodness that brightens up our world in the sense of creation, and goodness brightens our souls as believers. We have come to the light! Jesus is the incarnate Word of God who has come as the light that enlightens all people (John 1:4–14). *"GOD IS LIGHT and no shadow of darkness can exist in Him"* (1 John 1:5, PHILLIPS). Believing and receiving the truth, we are set free to bear fruit.

> You are the light of the world. A town built on a hill cannot be hidden. Neither do people light a lamp and put it under a bowl. Instead they put it on its stand, and it gives light to everyone in the house. *In the same way, let your light shine before others*, that they may see your *good* deeds and glorify your Father in heaven. (Matthew 5:14–16, emphasis added)

Lord Jesus, today I answer this call to let my light shine. Where I have been reluctant, please forgive me. I want the world to watch how I live my life and be led to you. In your name I pray. Amen.

A Moment of Truth

Day Twenty-Eight
Contributed by Jeeva Sam

In everything set them an example by doing what is good.
In your teaching show integrity, seriousness and soundness
of speech that cannot be condemned ... (Titus 2:7–8a)

It was one of the most difficult moments in our marriage up to that point. I had to fess up to Sulojana, my wife of thirty years, that I had built up a mountain of debt without her knowledge. Not from gambling or any vices, nor by indulging in unnecessary luxuries or satisfying other fleshly desires. I had simply chosen to live beyond our means, investing in certain programs and projects that promised to produce additional income streams. I justified them as "good" debt. But when the anticipated income didn't exceed the actual output, this was the outcome.

The look on Sulojana's face showed how shocked she was at the amount. It was more than our annual income at the time. I hung my head in shame as she expressed her dismay, disappointment, frustration, and anger. My choices had fallen outside the integrity pathway by hiding the truth until now. While I was truly repentant, the best I could say was, "I'm so sorry. I take full responsibility for what I did. Will you forgive me?"

Then came the dreaded pause. It was awfully long, not to mention awkward. I waited with bated breath. I deserved whatever was coming, but she delivered the blow in a measured tone with no loud outbursts. She said she needed some time to process what I had just shared. Not surprising, since Sulojana is wired to be a contemplator.

On the one hand, I expected that as a born-again, Holy Spirit-led follower of Jesus, she would forgive me. She wouldn't act rashly. She would seek the wisdom of God in her quiet time before giving me a response.

On the other hand, I was also aware that in situations such as this, it's easy to respond out of hurt. As a pastor, I've seen many godly men and women, even leaders, inflict greater hurt upon those who hurt them. Our spirits may alert us that forgiveness is the right response, but we could easily override those spiritual instincts with soulish impulses. It's in us to feel the need to administer justice, as we see it, and sometimes even payback. Perhaps you can relate.

What would Sulojana decide?

After what seemed like an eternity (more like twenty-four hours on an earthly clock), she returned and said, "Jeeva, as you could tell, I was not at all happy with what you did, because your choices have placed our family in a financially precarious position. But we cannot undo the past. What we can do is see how we can pay off the debt. Let's begin by praying together and seeking what the Lord wants us to do."

Phew! To say that I was relieved would be an understatement. I was overwhelmed by the goodness shown in her response. Faced with fleshly alternatives, she chose to forgive and find a way to move forward. In other words, she chose to *"Trust in the Lord and do good"* (Psalm 37:3a). She wouldn't allow the circumstance to dictate her response, but the fruit of the Spirit and obedience to the Word. God, in His grace, reminded me always to set a godly example by doing what is good in His sight, thus representing Him well in both wisdom and integrity.

Postscript: As we implemented Holy Spirit-inspired strategies and applied biblical counsel from financial advisors, the mountain of debt disappeared, and walking in financial freedom became the norm.

Heavenly Father, continue to teach me how to live in the integrity that can never be condemned. I choose to cultivate the fruit of the Spirit in my life so that I am always growing in your grace. Amen.

Finding a Good, Good Father

Day Twenty-Nine
Contributed by Belma Vardy

You are good, and what you do is good; teach me your decrees. (Psalm 119:68)

I'm often encouraged as I read the biblical record of a young Timothy, who needed a caring and committed "coach" to walk alongside him in his spiritual journey. The apostle Paul was travelling around the Roman Empire to plant churches and spread the gospel. Timothy was allowed to join him in his missionary journeys and grow in his faith. Paul mentored Timothy in how to be a faithful and effective minister of the gospel, how to deal with false teachers and persecution, and how to handle relationships. Timothy became his son in the faith.

When I taught at the First Nations Bible College in Vancouver, I met a student by the name of Lloyd. His story really impacted my life. Lloyd's journey testifies to the powerful work of God's kindness and goodness in transforming a life of addiction and pain.

Lloyd lived on the street for twelve years. Rocking back and forth in a fetal position on the sidewalk, burning with his most recent fix, he remembers crying out, "I want a father. I wish I had a father." Lloyd had no idea who he was speaking to or whether anyone was listening.

Someone walking by said, "I'll take you to meet the Father, but first you need to be introduced to His Son." That invitation was the beginning of a God-ordained father/son partnership. This man (we'll call him M) walked beside Lloyd, brought him to salvation, took care of him, and mentored him for the next number of years. Lloyd received a deep revelation of his Father's love, a good Father who sacrificed His own Son to bring Lloyd the gift of forgiveness and new life.

M helped Lloyd to acquire a job in janitorial services, doing cleaning during the night shifts. Lloyd was fathered on how to stay clean, how to walk in restored health, and how to build life-giving relationships.

Fast track forward: Lloyd had graduated his third year of Bible college when I met him. He's now ordained and works as assistant pastor in Vancouver's downtown east side. As a volunteer at Potter's Place Mission, he spends hours praying with street people and spreading the love of Jesus wherever he goes. His message to them all is, "God is my everything!"

God's goodness broke Lloyd free from the chains of addiction and brought him to First Nations Bible College. God connected Lloyd and me so that I could help him write his story. And now Lloyd reaches others with freedom and hope. Our God is so faithful!

The stories of both Timothy and Lloyd display God's kindness and goodness through actions. Lloyd grew in understanding how to live out what is upright and righteous.

Let's ask God to make us sensitive to those who need that hand up. May God show us where we can be used by Him to display his goodness: "*Whoever brings blessing will be enriched, and one who waters will himself be watered*" (Proverbs 11:25, ESV).

Dear Lord, give me strength for the long haul so that I don't become weary or faint-hearted in serving others. Fill me with wisdom and love to help others rise to freedom and victory. In Jesus' name. Amen.

Reflecting on His Goodness

Day Thirty

Surely your goodness and love will follow me all the days of my life, and I will dwell in the house of the Lord forever.
(Psalm 23:6)

I'm sure that as you come to our thirtieth day of devotionals focusing on "embracing goodness," you'll agree that each has been unique and inspiring. Each contributor has come from a place of authenticity and honesty to share their story with you. The stories are real, and they are heartfelt. The testimonies and biblical reviews vary, but the outworking of goodness expressed by each contributor is fragrant with gratitude. There is as well something else they all have in common—they add to the ever-growing mountain of evidence that goodness is alive and well!

I hope that while reading through the devotionals, you could select any day, in sequence or out of sequence, and find a story to uplift, encourage, and challenge you to reflect on the goodness of God that you have experienced in your own life. I hope you've done lots of highlighting and filled the margins with notes! I pray that you'll believe afresh that Christlikeness, expressed through your life, can bring change, healing, and freedom to people in your sphere of influence. May you be stirred to embrace biblical goodness as foundational to every decision and action.

Today I have provided a space for reflection. Write your recent or well-loved testimony of gratitude for God's goodness. If you're reading with a group of friends, share your story with them. If not, share it with a family member or simply offer it as praise to the Lord. You may prefer to use the space to make note of God's goodness in your daily routines over the next week. Following your personal reflection, you'll find a series of quotations on goodness. Consider how they may apply to your life, or travel slowly and simply allow your spirit to be built up and strengthened as you read through them.

Quotations for Reflection

"Do all the good you can, by all the means you can, in all the ways you can, in all the places you can, at all the times you can, to all the people you can, as long as ever you can."

—John Wesley

"The goodness of God is infinitely more wonderful than we will ever be able to comprehend."

—Aiden Wilson Tozer

"To be grateful is to recognize the Love of God in everything He has given us - and He has given us everything. Every breath we draw is a gift of His love, every moment of existence is a grace, for it brings with it immense graces from Him. Gratitude therefore takes nothing for granted, is never unresponsive, is constantly awakening to new wonder and to praise of the goodness of God. For the grateful person knows that God is good, not by hearsay but by experience. And that is what makes all the difference."

—Thomas Merton

"Remember the goodness of God in the frost of adversity."

—Charles Spurgeon

"The very first temptation in the history of mankind was the temptation to be discontent … that is exactly what discontent(ment) is—a questioning of the goodness of God."

—Jerry Bridges

"Do not look for evil. Look for the goodness of God all around you. As you look for signs of His Presence, many more opportunities will occur for you to bless people and share God's true nature."

—*Graham Cooke*

"Whatever may be the mysteries of life and death, there is one mystery which the cross of Christ reveals to us, and that is the infinite and absolute goodness of God. Let all the rest remain a mystery so long as the mystery of the cross of Christ gives us faith for all the rest."

—*Charles Kingsley*

"Jesus is not your accuser ... He's your friend and your rescuer. Like Zacchaeus, just spend time with Jesus. Don't hide from him in shame or reject him in self-righteousness. Don't allow the opinions of other people to shape your concept of him. Get to know him for yourself, and let the goodness of God change you from the inside out."

—*Judah Smith*[7]

"Beloved, I say, let your fears go, lest they make you fainthearted. Stop inspiring fear in those around you and now take your stand in faith. God has been good and He will continue to manifest His goodness. Let us approach these days expecting to see the goodness of the Lord manifest. Let us be strong and of good courage, for the Lord will fight for us if we stand in faith."

—*Francis Frangipane*[8]

"The greater your knowledge of the goodness and grace of God on your life, the more likely you are to praise Him in the storm."

—*Matt Chandler*[9]

---

[7] Above quotations taken from "Christian Quotes," AZ Quotes, accessed December 8, 2023, https://www.azquotes.com/quotes/topics/christian.html.

[8] "30 Francis Frangipane Quotes," Christian Quotes, accessed December 22, 2023, https://www.christianquotes.info/quotes-by-author/francis-frangipane-quotes/.

[9] "40 Christian Quotes to Encourage and Guide You on Your Daily Walk," Parade, accessed December 8, 2023, https://parade.com/living/christian-quotes.

Reflections

EMBRACING GOODNESS

64

Small Group Helps

This devotional journey welcomes the participation of others in a small group setting, either in person or online. There are three suggested ways to read with your group.

1. A four-week group session, meeting once weekly. By having the group read one extra entry on weeks three and four, you can complete the journey in the four weeks.
2. A five-week session, reading one devotional daily but taking Sundays off.
3. A six-week session, reading five devotionals each week, taking the weekends off.

Each participant will need their own copy of the book and can journal any takeaways or questions from their daily readings. In a small group setting, all participants should be reading the devotional entries at the same time so that discussions centre around the same readings on any given week. Discussing your insights will reveal some impacting and exciting truths.

The group leader may select two to five questions from the following list for the weekly group meeting, which should run about one hour. Vary your selection of questions from the list, adapting them to your group's focus. Be sure to allow time for personal thoughts, testimonies of growth, and any questions. Keep a scriptural view as foundational, and expect God to meet with you as you gather. The preferred leadership style for this topic is facilitation, where the leader encourages both participation and time boundaries during sharing. The facilitator should be familiar with the material and keep the discussion moving.

General Discussion Questions

(Choose your own adventure!)

These questions are suitable for use any week.

1. Which biblical character or event was most impactful to your growth this week?

2. What life lesson did you learn from that character or event?

3. Which testimony stood out for you this week? Share what you gained from it.

4. Share one truth from this week's readings that might be relevant to pass along to a specific friend for discussion in the future.

5. Choose a scripture verse from this week's devotionals and unpack what it means in your life right now.

6. Talk about your greatest goodness challenge right now and pray for one another.

Specific Questions Listed by Day

DAY ONE
- Share some thoughts about an "unlikely" biblical character whom God used.

- Do you see yourself as one of God's unlikely people? Share your thoughts.

DAY TWO
- Have you ever participated in a benevolent activity that brought others and yourself great joy? Share the testimony of God at work.

- In what way has God changed a challenge in your personal life into a testimony?

DAY THREE
- Share with the group a dark or difficult time in your life when you experienced God's goodness.

- Kerrin says, "As He revealed my pattern of striving and its resulting damage, He showed me that I did not have to keep 'doing' to earn the love and acceptance I already had from Him." Is this something that many of us experience, and if so, why?

DAY FOUR
- Do we as believers have what it takes to do right when the world demands that everyone make his own interests a priority?

- Mark 7:32–36 serves to remind me that if there's truly any goodness we have to offer the world, it won't be something that can just be mustered up from within. Explain.

DAY FIVE
- "I realize as well that it was the Holy Spirit who stirred Carl to get up early every Sunday, brush the snow off that bus, gas it up, and pick up a couple of dozen wild and energetic kids on each Sunday morning run. He did this with integrity and selflessness." Have you ever experienced God giving you a "hidden" task that required integrity, selflessness, and patience? Share with the group.

- Discuss today's scripture verse, Hebrews 13:16

DAY SIX
- Talk with your group about the importance of the role Barnabas played in the record of New Testament letters we have today.

- Balcony people believe change, with God's help, is possible. Discuss some of the characteristics or character traits of a "Barnabas" and why each one is important.

DAY SEVEN

- Has God ever used your house in the midst of someone's storm?

- Part of today's prayer is, "*I ask today, Lord God, that you would expand the walls of my heart and my home to show the goodness you have showered upon me.*" What might it look like for you when God answers that prayer?

DAY EIGHT

- What do you think these statements mean? "Generous giving is the outflow of all who give themselves first to the Lord. Personal response to God's goodness to us brings with it practical expression."

- Discuss this statement from today's story. "No one would have argued that they'd done a 'good' thing if they just offered their own guitar. But the integrity of heart matters. They knew the 'right' thing to do." Is there a personal experience you would like to share?

DAY NINE

- Do you have a friend or family member who is in the pit of pain and doesn't want your prayers? How do you handle this?

- Have you ever had a powerful visitation from the Lord like Randy did? Share the testimony of God's goodness with the group.

DAY TEN

- Wade describes his experience when coming to know Christ in this way: "The presence of God was so strong in that tent that I began to weep. It was like the liquid love of Jesus pouring all over me. I was experiencing true love for the first time in my life." Share your experience of salvation with the group.

- Which fruit of the Spirit (i.e., peace, patience, kindness, self-control, love, faithfulness, joy, goodness) needs to be cultivated in your personal life so that you can be a light to others in the healing process?

DAY ELEVEN

- 2 Kings 22:2 introduces Josiah by saying, *"He did what was right in the eyes of the Lord ... not turning aside to the right or to the left."* One of the "right" things he did was to repent and make changes that would glorify God. How significant was that action and why?

- How am I displaying in my place of influence the character of the good and loving God whom I serve?

DAY TWELVE

- In Ephesians 5, Paul states that believers should be imitators of God and that they are children of light. How is Christ shining through you?

- Sherry says, "Each child will have distinctive characteristics that reveal who their parents are." What is unique in how He has "wired" you to express His goodness?

DAY THIRTEEN

- When Jennifer says, "By *repositioning my heart to receive this new challenge as a good gift from my Heavenly Father,* I was able to look beyond my feelings and find the strength to persevere." What do you do when you face a new challenge?

- How do you war against worry in your life?

DAY FOURTEEN

- Identify some of the places in Fanny Crosby's journey where you see God's goodness manifest.

- Though Fanny could have been bitter and resentful, she didn't let her physical disability stop her from praising God and sharing His goodness and love with others. What do you think holds us back when we have freedom to worship and praise Him?

DAY FIFTEEN
- Julie tells us that a time came on their journey when they became curious about how God would show His goodness during their mess. They fluctuated between faith and distress. Have you ever been there in your Christian walk? How do you relate?

- Have you ever been blessed to meet a (Mrs. or) Mr. Smiley? Share the experience as a testimony for your group.

DAY SIXTEEN
- In a world full of pain, disease, injustice, and confusion, Jesus brought goodness. What does that mean for us today?

- How can this Day Sixteen devotional be a good news story? It seems anything but good.

DAY SEVENTEEN
- In the parable of the Good Samaritan, Jesus paints a picture that makes it very clear how to respond to the needs that come our way. What instruction does He give us?

- Discuss these statements. "No human law will compel you to cross over to the person in that ditch or step into that struggle that you'll meet later this week. But if you do—if you choose to move toward the pain of others rather than around it—you will be walking the way of Jesus."

DAY EIGHTEEN
- What do you do when you are in a season where you can't "feel" God?

- Share with your group what you think John Ortberg is saying in this quotation: "Prayer becomes real when we grasp the reality and goodness of God's constant presence with 'the real me.'"

DAY NINETEEN

- Have you ever found yourself in the Romans 7 struggle Paul talks about? What helps to bring your mind to a place of rest when this happens?

- "There can be no progress in cultivating goodness or righteous living until we learn what Paul learned here—that in me (that is, in my flesh) lives nothing good." Spend some time unpacking this with your group.

DAY TWENTY

- What do you think today's scripture means? *"Oh, how great is Your goodness, which You have laid up for those who fear You, which You have prepared for those who trust in You in the presence of the sons of men!"* (Psalm 31:19, NKJV).

- While Amenla was busy obeying God's call, He was putting everything in place to bless her with the desire of her heart. Have you ever had God work behind the scenes while you were moving on in obedience in His call to you?

DAY TWENTY-ONE

- What are some of the dangers of apathy in our lives?

- How does being transformed/changed fall into the category of God's goodness?

DAY TWENTY-TWO

- Suggest some ways that we can process pain in a healthy, biblical manner.

- How much do you believe He's working on your behalf, even when you're not aware of it? Share with the group a personal testimony of His work behind the scenes.

DAY TWENTY-THREE

- Discuss the interesting definition of grace unpacked in today's devotional.

- How do you feel when you pause to consider that you are the object of His affection, and because of His divine nature, all that He expresses comes from an abundant, God-sized goodness toward you?

DAY TWENTY-FOUR

- Has there been a special milestone in your life where you have clearly seen God's goodness?

- Cherie says, "I can't change the diagnosis or the circumstances for my patients, but I can brighten their day in some way. God shows me how to anticipate their needs, gives me empathy, kindness, and love for those in my care. He gives me the right words to say when courage is needed, and the energy to go the extra mile to serve those in a time of need. God is a God of love—and miracles still happen!" How might this also apply in your situation?

DAY TWENTY-FIVE

- The goodness of God in Marion and Jake's life interrupted the plan of the enemy. What plans might He have interrupted in your life to show you His goodness?

- Sometimes we have trauma upon trauma, disappointment upon disappointment, and loss upon loss. Do you think this makes the healing process more difficult? Why or why not?

DAY TWENTY-SIX

- Has there ever been a Michael in your life who was instrumental in bringing you to Jesus? Share with the group.

- In what specific area of your life does this verse hold meaning for you right now? "... *I am the light of the world: he that followeth me shall not walk in darkness, but shall have the light of life*" (John 8:12, KJV).

DAY TWENTY-SEVEN

- Share some favourite spots in the Christmas story where you can identify God's goodness.

- "Light signifies God's goodness that brightens up our world in the sense of creation, and goodness brightens our souls as believers—we have come to the light." Explain and discuss.

DAY TWENTY-EIGHT

- Jeeva felt that he wasn't representing God with honesty and integrity by keeping his secret. Is he right? Why or why not?

- Jeeva warns, "Our spirits may alert us that forgiveness is the rightful response. However, we could easily override those spiritual instincts with soulish impulses. It's in us to feel the need to administer justice, as we see it, and sometimes even payback. Perhaps you can relate ..." How do you relate?

DAY TWENTY-NINE

- How important is it to have another believer show us the heart of the Father?

- M provided a lot of different kinds of help to Lloyd. What was the significance of this in helping him to be strengthened in the Christian walk?

DAY THIRTY

- Choose a quotation about goodness from those listed at the end of Day Thirty. Unpack it for the group.

- Now that you have finished the devotional readings, share your understanding of what you believe goodness means from a biblical perspective.

About the Author

Ruth Teakle lives with her husband, Carl, in Grimsby, Ontario. She loves to spend time with her three children and their spouses and her eleven grandchildren. Although retired, Ruth serves as a support staff member at Lakemount Worship Centre in Grimsby, Ontario, where she previously served on full-time and part-time staff for over twenty years. Her roles varied from overseeing small groups and missions to prayer and pastoral care. As well, she has led and assisted with numerous short-term missions to the Caribbean, Eastern Europe, Ukraine, South America, northern Ontario, and Quebec.

Ruth has worked within the Correctional Services of Canada, volunteered with numerous summer camp programs through both Girls Guides of Canada and the Salvation Army, directed an annual city-wide Christmas toy program, and filmed a national training course for telephone prayer partners. She also served for many years in local, area, and national capacities with Aglow International Canada prior to pastoral ministry.

Ruth's academic pursuits have included studies at Lakeshore Teachers' College, Brock University (Bachelor of Arts), and Wagner University (Master of Practical Ministries). She has completed ESL studies and is a Certified Anger Management Specialist and Trauma Healing Master Facilitator. Prior to taking additional Religious Studies courses with Global University in preparation for ordained ministry, Ruth enjoyed a successful thirty-two-year career as an elementary school teacher.

Ruth is an ordained minister with the Pentecostal Assemblies of Canada and has a heart to see people become passionate followers of Christ. She also has a strong sense of mission to help disciple them into healthy connections with God and others. Her challenging but victorious personal journey makes her well-qualified to share on the importance of cultivating the fruit of the Spirit in one's life.

Additional Note: Ruth's first devotional, *Changing Seasons*, is a pocket/purse-sized devotional full of encouragement from God's Word written especially for seniors, and it's one of the GODQUEST SERIES available only through The Bible League, Canada.

bibleleague.ca/resources/godquest/

Pursuing Patience, Pursuing Peace, Choosing Love, Choosing Kindness, Cultivating Faith, Experiencing Joy and Cultivating Gentleness and Self-Control are available through Word Alive Press and numerous national and international outlets including Amazon and Indigo.

Ruth's Christian Education curriculum for students in grades four to seven, published in 2023, is available through Amazon.ca and Amazon.com. It's titled *Growing My Faith: A Study for Elementary Students Encouraging Moral Excellence, Behavioural Change and Productive Community.* An accompanying *Growing My Faith: Manual for Teachers* is also available, containing over fifty classroom and group activities to support the student manual.

Ruth has also authored a delightfully illustrated children's book for children ages four to nine, *Joshua Wonders: What Does the Tooth Fairy Do with My Teeth?* available through numerous national and international outlets, including Amazon and Indigo.

Contributor Biographies

RANDY COCKHEAD

Randy Cockhead was born and continues to live in Niagara Falls, Ontario. He's been married for forty-six years to his wife, Diane, and together they have two sons, who make them very proud.

Having served in numerous capacities in the local church and the community, Randy has seen the hand of God work in many miraculous ways throughout his life. After many years in the industrial field, Randy now enjoys a life of retirement as a grandfather to three. Randy has a passion for the Word and prayer, and a great love for Jesus.

MARK AND NICOLETTE CULLEN

Mark Cullen was born in Bournemouth, England; Nicolette was born in Cape Town, South Africa. By God's infinite grace and divine intervention, they met in Burlington, Ontario in 2000.

They are active in their community in various volunteer roles and in their church family at Lakemount Worship Centre, where they've served for the past fourteen years. This has included short-term missions, guest services, outreach, and life groups. Nicolette has over fifteen years of experience in event planning and floral arranging as owner of Petals and Parties.

This past July 2023, Mark and Nicolette celebrated twenty years of marriage. They reside in Grimsby, Ontario and have been blessed with two daughters, a son, and three grandchildren. They enjoy camping, family time, and travelling.

AMENLA CUNNINGHAM

Pastor Amenla Cunningham was born in Nagaland, Northeast India. She pastors alongside her husband as Women's Pastor at First Assemblies of God, Bangalore. She's a prayer warrior; her passion is to raise spiritual mothers for the EKKLESIA and empower women to discover their destiny in God. She served in All India AG Women's Ministry for fourteen years and was convenor for Women of Destiny Inter-denominational Prayer Movement Bangalore and Anti-Human Trafficking Network Bangalore.

Amenla also serves as Director for Girls' Homes for those rescued from high-risk situations. Her passion is to serve Jesus with all her heart and see a mighty revival across the nations!
https://www.firstagchurch.in/.

JAN FINOCHIO

Jan Finochio serves in both pastoral and administrative roles at Crossroads Life Church in Harriston, Ontario and can always be found busy behind the scenes. Jan comes from a strong musical background and loves to worship. She finds fulfillment in caring for her home and family, sewing, and connecting with people. She's a great cook, and many people have been touched by her heart-warming gift of hospitality.

Jan has been married to John Finochio since 1979, and they have three grown children: Nathan, Gabriel, and Tiffany. John and Jan Finochio were installed as lead pastors of Crossroads Life Church in January of 2000. Since then, Crossroads has grown from a handful of people to a thriving family church embracing all ages. Jan and John have served with an international network of church leaders through Minister's Fellowship International (MFI) for over two decades.
https://mfileader.org/
https://www.youtube.com/c/crossroadslifechurch.

JENNIFER HAY

Jennifer Hay is a pastor with the PAOC and currently serving as the Centre Director at Teen Challenge's Ontario Women's Centre. The centre provides a twelve-month in-residence alcohol and drug addiction rehabilitation program for adults eighteen and older in the Greater Toronto Area. Jennifer's heart is to serve those in her sphere of influence and to make an impact on the lives of women seeking healing and empowerment.

With a passion for teaching the Bible, she has led countless Bible studies both in person and online. Whether she's serving her church or community, Jennifer is a beacon of hope, encouragement, and support.

Jennifer is an avid sports fan who can be found cheering on the Toronto Blue Jays and the Barrie Colts. She lives in Innisfil, Ontario with her husband, Bryan, and their daughter, Abigail. **https://www.tcgta.ca/.**

CHERIE MARTIN

Cherie Martin is a Registered Nurse at the Hospital for Sick Children in Toronto and a private nurse for two beautiful girls in the Niagara Region. She has been married for over twenty years to her amazing husband, Pete, and is a mom of three awesome "kids" (Jodey, Aliah, and Caden) and a new mother-in-law to Wolfe (Jodey's husband).

Cherie loves Jesus, loves being a nurse, and has enjoyed every phase and stage of being a mom. She's now learning to parent adult children and to explore a little more freedom, enjoying the outdoors, walking her puppy, gardening, kayaking, volleyball, and photography.

KERRIN NORMAN

Since Kerrin Norman came to know Jesus at forty, she's been passionate about the Word of God and serving in her local church. She loves to express worship as she creates through various art forms. Kerrin graduated from a two-year ministry internship, and God has used her passion for Him to encourage others. Sharing what God has done for her and seeing other women walk in the freedom always brings her great joy. She thrives in organizational areas, hospitality, and prayer ministry. Jesus is at the heart of who Kerrin is.

Kerrin lives with her husband, Ken, and daughter, Avery, in Smithville, Ontario. In her spare time, she loves to read, hike, and get out on her motorcycle.

JEEVA SAM

Jeeva Sam and his wife of forty years, Sulojana, are marriage mentors and co-authors of *The Unbreakable Marriage*.

Jeeva served as pastor to both Morgan's Point and Forks Road East United Churches in Wainfleet Township in the Niagara Region prior to his retirement in 2017. At that time, he had completed thirty-five years of pastoral ministry.

Along with the marriage mentorship, Jeeva presently serves as a spiritual, personal, relational, and business mentor to leaders in the marketplace. The Sams are parents of three married children and grandparents of a newborn baby boy. They live in the Niagara Region of Canada. **www.thesams.ca.**

WADE AND JENNY SANDERSON

Wade and Jenny Sanderson live in Martensville, Saskatchewan and have been married since 2019. They have a handsome three-year-old son, Maranatha.

Wade and Jenny met through a Bible college program and founded Inspire Fire Ministries in 2021. Through their ministry, they serve as evangelists, bringing the hope, love, and power of Jesus to Indigenous communities and beyond. They've travelled across Canada and abroad to preach the gospel and pray for the sick and those trapped in addictions. They're also involved in reconciliation efforts between the Indigenous and non-Indigenous people in Canada, believing that God can heal the wounds of the past and bring unity, healing, and peace.

In their free time, Wade enjoys fishing, and Jenny loves nature and worshipping!

https://www.facebook.com/InspireFireMinistries/

SHERRY STAHL

Sherry Stahl is an inspirational Bible teacher, author, speaker, and blogger. As a speaker certified with the John Maxwell Team, you'll often find Sherry amusing audiences at conferences, women's events, and business training seminars. She's the founder of Soul H2O Ministries and lives to help others find the life-giving water in God's Word that has so often quenched her weary soul.

Sherry loves to travel and view the world from the back of Todd's Harley. She has authored two amazing devotionals, *Water in the Desert* and *SoulH2O*. You can find her online at **www.sherrystahl.com.**

JULIE STAUTLAND

Julie Stautland, a first runner-up to Miss Teen Canada 1985, is a co-founder with her husband, Tore, of The News Forum Network and Trillennium Media Group Inc.

She met her husband while performing and travelling with an international Christian theatre ministry. Once they settled in Canada, she spent several years as a youth leader and worship leader in their local church. She also enjoyed time as a motivational speaker in schools, Christian conferences, and events, sharing her testimony. Julie became a stay–at–home mom, homeschooling their two beautiful daughters through high school.

In Julie's book, *TRAUMA QUEEN: A Broken Beauty Discovers God's Love*, she shares her journey and victories through her battles with eating disorders, depression, and sexual abuse.

Julie is currently a guest news anchor for *Forum Daily News*. In her spare time, she enjoys fencing and paddleboarding. She treasures time at her remote office or prayer closest.

juliestautland.com.
https://www.thenewsforum.ca/.

MEGHAN VANDERKRUK

Meghan Vanderkruk is a lover of sports, nutrition, and most of all, Jesus. She uses her degree in kinesiology to train athletes and choreograph competitive dancers. She loves using her skills to encourage the next generation, sharing her story to connect with them on a heart level.

Meghan volunteers on the leadership team at Lakemount Young Adults. She has a burden for her generation and loves serving by designing merchandise for evangelism, building vision for social media, and leading the content team. She often serves as the Young Adults service host.

At World Vision Canada, she works with a committed Christian team that partners to advocate for and deliver aid to people living in dangerous places.

https://www.worldvision.ca/about-us.

BELMA VARDY

Belma Vardy in an inspirational speaker and founder of the Celebration of Dance ministry. Her ministry aims to foster intimacy with God through teaching, encouragement, worship, and movement.

For over thirty years, Belma has traversed the globe, inspiring people of all ages and denominations to discover deeper experiences of the Father's love. She has appeared as a guest on various Christian TV programs and podcasts. She has also served as the National Coordinator for the Christian Dance Fellowship of Canada and International Joint-Coordinator for Children's Dance Ministries, based out of Australia.

Her compelling personal journey is recorded in her book *Because God Was There: A Journey of Loss, Healing and Overcoming.* Her most recent book, *Because the Spirit was There: Windows into First Nations Communities*, documents stories and experiences of our First Nations communities that deliver hope and healing through the truth of our identity in God.

https://www.celebrationofdance.com/